Power Desserts

the ultimate collection of nutrition-
packed, reduced-fat indulgences

KGL

by Karen L. Pellegrin

CHAMPION PRESS, LTD.
FREDONIA, WISCONSIN

CHAMPION PRESS, LTD.
FREDONIA, WISCONSIN

Cover Design by Fineman Communications

ISBN: 1891400568
LCCN: 2003110336

Manufactured in the United States of America 10 9 8 7 6 5 4

Praise for Power Desserts

"Think you can't have your wellness plan and eat dessert too? In her newest book, *Power Desserts*, Karen Pellegrin shows us yet again that eating healthy doesn't have to mean limiting your options. From Peanut Butter Brownies to Cream Cheese Pound Cake to Black Forest Pie, you'll find your traditional favorites as well as some new delicacies that are sure to make it onto your list of must-haves. Indeed, you can have your cake—and even eat it, too!" **Carrie Myers Smith, co-founder and president, Women in Wellness; contributing editor and columnist, *Energy for Women* magazine; and author of *Squeezing Your Size 14 Self into a Size 6 World***

"As a Registered Dietitian, I'm always looking for that combination of good taste and good nutrition. These are the best desserts I've ever tasted and what a bonus to be so packed with nutrients!" **Eileen Stellefson Myers, MPH, RD, FADA**

"Well I have to admit that I was skeptical about low-fat, low-cholesterol, reduced-calorie dessert recipes tasting even remotely like desserts. I was glad to be proven wrong with this delightful book. Each one of the desserts has significantly less fat (often one third less), has almost completely eliminated the cholesterol, and has added nutrients and minerals. I have always equated less fat with less taste simply because that has been my experience, now I can say that less fat can still mean delicious." **Harold McFarland, Editor, Readers Preference Reviews**

"Power Desserts is the answer to a 'sweet tooth's' prayer! The pages are filled with luscious desserts that are not only good tasting, but good for you." **Arlene Shovald, Ph.D. author of** *Arlene's Cuisine, The Mountain Mail* **newspaper, Salida, Colorado**

"Power Desserts adds a whole new dimension to everybody's favorite part of dinner by not only cutting the calories, but making the desserts nutritious as well. What better way to get your daily dietary requirements than with German Chocolate Cake, Raspberry Lemon Pie or Oatmeal Cranberry Cookies? Detailed nutrition boxes back up the claim of healthy baking." **Myrna Collins, Cookbook Reviewer, The Post Crescent**

Acknowledgements...

In memory of my Mom, Judy Pellegrin...
Brave Adventurer
Eternal Optimist
Multi-media Artist
Zealous Social Director
Devoted Friend
Joyous Mother
"Love never dies"

Special thanks to:

All those who helped with this book by tasting my new recipes, but especially the staff at the VA Hospital Mental Health Services administration in Charleston, South Carolina for being such enthusiastic and reliable guinea pigs.

Chris Frueh, my husband and Chief Recipe Tester, for protecting the other taste-testers from the duds and for being the sweetest part of my sugary sweet life.

My dad, Gene Pellegrin, and my sisters, Lauren Wetter and Becky Padavan, for all your support and for patiently listening to my fanatical health sermons. You have always been precious to me, now more than ever.

Brook Noel at Champion Press for investing in this project and in me.

What Are "Power Desserts"?

Power Desserts are as much about attitude as they are about ingredients. The attitude behind Power Desserts is one of zest for life. This zest fuels the desire to do the things that will protect your health and safety, such as eating right, exercising, getting check-ups, and wearing seatbelts. But it is this same zest that also inspires the wisdom to see that quality of life is more important than quantity and that, no matter how long you live, life's too short not to enjoy it every minute that you can. So, do the things you can do to reduce the risk of early death or illness, but don't give up the things that make life worth living. Take a bike ride, but wear a helmet; go to the beach, but wear sunscreen; enjoy a drink with family and friends, but don't drive; and save room for dessert, but make it a Power Dessert!

How are Power Desserts different? Regular desserts have been maligned for two primary reasons: 1) they contain lots of bad fats that can lead to heart disease and other health problems, and 2) they are "empty calories" – that is, they contain nothing good for you. Power Desserts are:

1) **Reduced fat** – all of the unhealthy fats have been taken out or radically reduced. This means there are no butter, egg yolks, cream, etc. Some of the recipes are fat-free. Those recipes that contain any

1

significant amount of fat, get that fat mostly from the healthy oils in nuts.

2) **Excellent source of nutrients** – each recipe contains at least 20% of the daily value of one or more nutrients, at least one ounce of a food high in anti-oxidants, at least 0.5 gram of Omega-3 fatty acids, and/or at least 5 grams of Omega-6 fatty acids. (Nutritional analyses of each recipe were conducted using The Food Processor® software by ESHA Research.)

3) **Easy** – These recipes are mostly simple to follow and not very time-consuming. No sifting, no double boilers, no fuss!

4) **Delicious!**

For example, let's compare how traditional recipes stack up to Power Desserts for a same-size serving:

German Chocolate Cake

	Traditional	Power Dessert (see p. 54)
Calories	645	405
Total fat	34 g	7 g
% of calories from fat	48%	15%
Saturated fat	9 g	1 g
Cholesterol	75 mg	1 mg
Calcium	86 mg	221 mg

Chocolate Chip Cookies

	Traditional	Power Dessert (see p. 22)
Calories	543	351
Total fat	32 g	9 g
% of calories from fat	51%	23%
Saturated fat	14 g	2 g
Cholesterol	73 mg	0 mg
Iron	1.7 mg	4.6

In a nutshell, Power Desserts offer "More Bang for the Bite!" They are also usually lower in calories, fat, and cholesterol compared to traditional desserts.

2. How to Benefit from Power Desserts

I've always had a sweet tooth along with an enjoyment of creating new desserts. But I haven't always been a healthy eater. My wake-up call came at the ripe ol' age of 23, when my first cholesterol test came back high. While uncontrollable things, namely genes, contributed to this, my regular consumption of premium ice cream, cookies, and other sweets was not helping matters and was 100% under my control. I chose to take control of what I could.

I now feel lucky that I got this wake up call so early in life and in a way that was not immediately life-threatening (e.g., a heart attack). Many illnesses, including both heart disease and cancer, can progress silently for years with no warning signs. For example, many people with normal cholesterol readings suffer from heart disease. I've now had many years to correct the things I can and many years of normal cholesterol readings.

Since that time, I've kept a close eye on the latest research in health and nutrition, and I've modified my behaviors accordingly. My dessert recipes have reflected the changes I have made in my diet. The recipes in my first cookbook were focused on removing the unhealthiest part of desserts – saturated fat. At that time, there was a general focus on reducing overall fat intake. Over the years, an accumulation of studies has led scientists to the conclusion that there are more than just bad fats and neutral fats. They have found that some fats (such as the

4

oils in nuts and fish) are actually good for us, resulting in many positive health outcomes. In addition, there is now powerful evidence that anti-oxidants, found mostly in plant-based foods, play a critical role in keeping all parts of the body healthy. Finally, vitamins and minerals, such as calcium and folate, are also essential to optimal health. The Power Desserts in this cookbook reflect my desire to make every bite count nutritionally without sacrificing taste.

The Basics of a Healthy Diet

I've heard many people complain that there's no point to trying to eat a healthy diet because the experts are constantly changing their recommendations. While there is a kernel of truth to this, it is mostly an excuse. Scientists have always been searching for the factors that contribute to good health. The body of knowledge has indeed grown and sometimes changed. But many of the basics have been the same for many years, and many of the changes have been really just refinements rather than radical departures from previous recommendations. To avoid a rollercoaster lifestyle, stay off of the latest health fads that are based on one or two small studies or pseudo-science. One of the cornerstones of the scientific method is that results must be replicated over time before valid conclusions can be drawn. If you are having a hard time separating science from sales pitches consult with a registered dietitian and/or consider subscribing to one of the "health" newsletters published by an academic organization (my favorites are the University of California Berkeley Wellness Letter and the Tufts University Health and Nutrition Letter).

Here are some dietary guidelines for good health in adults:
1) Diet composition should be 45-65% of calories from carbohydrates, 20-35% of calories from fat, and 10-35% of calories from protein. (According to the

September 2002 report from the National
Academies' Institute of Medicine)

2) Minimize or eliminate the bad fats. Bad fats include
saturated fats, which are found mostly in animal
products such as meat and cheese, and trans fatty
acids. Trans fats are found in foods that contain
"hydrogenated" or "partially hydrogenated" oils.
Food companies use these types of oils to extend
the shelf life of their products. Currently it is difficult
to know how much trans fatty acids are in a food
because these fats are not required to be listed on
food labels. This will change as the Food and Drug
Administration has announced that it will require
nutrition labels, by 2006, to include a new line to
show the amount of trans fat per serving.

3) Consume the good fats (i.e., monounsaturated and
polyunsaturated fats), but especially Omega-3 fatty
acids and Omega-6 fatty acids. Nuts, vegetable
oils, flaxseed, and fish are the best sources of
healthy oils. The September 2002 report from the
National Academies' Institute of Medicine
recommends 1.1-1.6 grams of alpha-linolenic acid
(an Omega-3 fatty acid) and 12-17 grams of
linoleic acid (an Omega-6 fatty acid) per day.

4) Consume 25-35 grams of fiber per day.

5) Eat five to nine servings of fruits and vegetables per
day (according to the National Cancer Institute).
Choose produce with dark or bright colors, such as
blueberries, broccoli, carrots, and sweet potatoes,
which seem to be higher in antioxidants.

6) Don't eat more calories than you burn. If you do, you will gain weight. To lose weight, you need to burn more calories than you eat.

Why not just pop some vitamins each day? Sales of vitamins and supplements have soared as researchers have learned more about what nutrients are needed for optimal health and consumers look for an easy way to get these nutrients. But experts have cautioned that taking vitamins should always be a last resort for those who can't or won't consume nutrients naturally by eating a variety of healthy foods each day. The reason for this is two-fold. First, some research has shown that some vitamins or supplements provide no benefit, and some actually do harm. This includes those supplements that are "natural," which is a term that means nothing with regard to safety or effectiveness. Second, scientists are aware that there are many substances in foods, especially fruits and vegetables, that they have not yet identified. These unknown substances may work together with the known substances (such as beta carotene) to provide valuable health benefits. For these reasons, it is best to get most, if not all, of your nutrients from food.

Since this is a cookbook, the focus is on food and nutrition. However, you can't talk about a healthy lifestyle without talking about exercise. The research is crystal clear that exercise is essential for optimal mental and physical health and quality of life. A sound exercise program includes regular aerobic activity as well as strength training. But the good news from the research that has been done indicates that even a little bit of exercise (if you currently get none) has some positive health benefits, and that even activities that you might not think of as exercise (such as gardening) are good for you. But be sure to consult your physician before starting an exercise program.

How You Can Benefit from Power Desserts

Far too many people in this country eat too much bad fat, too many calories, and not enough good fats, fruits, vegetables, vitamins and minerals. If you are one of these people, you would likely benefit from substituting some of the unhealthy or "empty" foods currently in your diet with Power Desserts. However, if you simply add Power Desserts to your current diet, instead of replacing part of the diet, you will be adding not only nutrients, but also calories. The way to make the recipes in this book work for you is to make sure you skip the regular candy bar, cookies, or cake whenever you add a Power Dessert!

A Word on Personal Responsibility

As you should have figured out by now, I'm a big advocate of taking control-of and responsibility-for your life and your choices. So don't go overboard with Power Desserts or think that everything in this cookbook is good for everybody. Step one in taking responsibility for your health is to make sure you get a regular check up and screening for common diseases that can be treated. Then you should follow your doctor's or registered dietitian's advice regarding diet and exercise changes you may need to make. If you are hypertensive and need to follow a low sodium diet, make sure you use the sodium information in the nutritional analyses of these recipes to guide your decisions. Like regular desserts, these Power Desserts vary in sodium content. This is not a low sodium cookbook. Similarly, if you are diabetic, follow your doctor's advice regarding limiting total carbohydrates, and use the nutritional information provided in this book to guide your dessert choices. This is not a low carbohydrate cookbook. And so on! The point here is to make sure you take charge of your health, making decisions and changes that are best for you.

Power Baking

Power Desserts are created from a combination of the right ingredients and the right techniques. This chapter reviews these key elements.

Power Ingredients

It is not only what is taken out of a recipe (butter, cream, etc.), but also what is put in it that makes it a Power Dessert. The key ingredients in these recipes are all concentrated sources of nutrients. The following list highlights the important ingredients used in this cookbook.

Egg substitute: Most egg substitutes are 99% egg white. Look for brands that are fat-free (most are). Also make sure to look for brands with no seasonings of any type. Some list onion or garlic flavoring on the ingredients list. You don't want that in your desserts!

Fat-free dairy products: Sour cream, whole milk, cream cheese, whole yogurt and other dairy products are high in saturated fat. They are now available in fat-free versions.

Fat-free margarine: Because there is no oil in fat-free margarine, you can't use it to sauté or fry foods. But, used in small amounts in these Power Desserts, it adds butter flavoring.

9

"Concentrated" foods: Sweetened condensed milk, evaporated milk, and fruit juice concentrates are simply foods that have had some of the water removed. This process results in products that are rich in nutrients. Note: sweetened condensed milk and evaporated milk are NOT interchangeable.

Frozen fruit: Many of the recipes in this cookbook that use fruit call for frozen fruit (e.g., blueberries, raspberries). One of the benefits of frozen fruits (and vegetables) is that they are often more nutritious than fresh. This is because they are flash frozen at their peak, while fresh produce loses its nutrients rapidly while sitting on the shelf. The other benefits to using frozen fruits are that they are convenient to use and you can get them year-round.

Vanilla extract: Don't use imitation vanilla flavoring. Pure vanilla extract has a much better taste and is worth the extra cost.

Unsweetened cocoa powder: How do you make chocolate desserts chocolaty without adding the fat found in chocolate chips and baking chocolate? Use cocoa powder, as I do in the chocolate recipes in this book.

Blackstrap molasses: Unlike all other sweeteners (including regular molasses), blackstrap molasses is an excellent source of iron and calcium. However, it has a very strong flavor – I would not recommend it as a pancake syrup! When used in small amounts, it can add a very rich flavor along with its nutrients.

Nuts and seeds: The only high fat ingredients I use liberally in my recipes are nuts and seeds. This is because they are rich in the good fats, as well as other important nutrients.

Power Techniques

In regular desserts, the oils help keep the baked item evenly moist. When you remove, or greatly reduce the oil content of recipes, it requires other changes in the baking process to prevent the edges from drying out before the center is cooked. I use two strategies in all of the baked recipes in this book to keep them evenly moist: 1) decrease oven temperature by 25° relative to regular desserts, and 2) increase baking time. If you want to try to reduce the fat in some of your own recipes, try using these two techniques.

General Baking Tips

I've done a lot of baking over the years and have accumulated a handful of strategies and techniques that might help make baking more efficient and effective for you. These suggestions are listed below:

Sifting: If there is a good reason to sift flour, I'm not aware of it. I've never sifted flour for any of my recipes, and I'd suggest that you skip the sifting too. Life's too short!

Measuring technique: When measuring dry, powdery ingredients, pack them in the measuring tool. (e.g., powdered sugar, cocoa powder, etc.) Brown sugar should also be packed. The only exception to this rule is flour. Flour should be scooped up with a spoon and lightly sprinkled into the measuring cup, and then leveled off with a straight edge.

Measuring tools: Most measuring tools come in standard sizes. For example, measuring cups typically come in ¼, ⅓, ½, and 1 full cup. Consider investing in measuring tools that come in other sizes. For example, I've found ⅔, ¾, and

1 ½ cups. These sizes save time by reducing the number of times ingredients need to be measured. For example, a recipe that calls for ⅔ cup of sugar requires two measuring steps if a ⅓ cup is used, but only one step if a ⅔ up is used. It may sound like a small time-saver, but I'll take every extra minute I can find!

Mixers: Until recently, I had been using a nearly 10-year-old hand-held mixer. It worked fine, but I was tempted into buying a newer model, and I am so pleased I did. The model I have has beaters that look more like small wire whisks than regular beaters. They cut through stiff batter easily. In addition, this mixer has a "soft-start" that prevents the cloud of dust that can be caused when the dry ingredients get kicked up by starting a mixer. Finally, this mixer has a very quiet motor. The only down side to this great piece of equipment is that the beaters are so thin that not very much batter sticks to them, which means less batter that needs to be licked off of them!

The toothpick test: This really is a good way to tell if most cakes, breads, and muffins are done. If you stick a toothpick into the center of the dessert and remove it, it will be dry (with the exception of a few crumbs) when the dessert is done. If the pick has wet batter stuck to it, the dessert needs to bake longer.

The "bang-on-the-oven-door" test: The toothpick test does have a few drawbacks. First, you have to open the oven to use this test, which drops the oven temperature significantly. Second, it doesn't work well for desserts like pies and cheesecakes. So, I've developed the "bang on the oven door" test. Just turn on the oven light and gently tap your fist against the oven door. If the center of the dessert jiggles, the batter has not cooked sufficiently. If it does not jiggle, it is likely cooked in the center and the dessert is done.

Storage: To prevent these desserts from drying out, be sure to cover them with foil after they have cooled if you are serving them from the pan. Or transfer the dessert to a plastic storage container with a tight lid. Most of the desserts in this cookbook freeze well and can be thawed one serving at a time by popping them in the microwave for 10-30 seconds.

Cookies, Brownies & Bars

Toll-Free Chocolate Chip Cookies
Makes 24 Large Cookies

Ideveloped a fat-free chocolate chip cookie recipe almost 10 years ago that tastes remarkably like the traditional Toll House® cookies. My husband and our two oldest nephews, Justin and Daniel, love them. Then I tweaked my fat-free version to make it a Power Dessert. You have to make the chips a day in advance, but they are really easy to make. The addition of pine nuts, with their buttery texture, adds nutrients and a rich taste. You will like them even if you don't usually prefer nuts in your cookies. These cookies (not to mention the cookie dough) are delicious! In addition to the Power Punch nutrients listed below, each serving is a good source of the following (based on percent of Daily Values): 16% of protein, 13% of riboflavin/B2, 10% of niacin/B3, 12% of folate, 19% of copper, 16% of magnesium, 12% of phosphorus, 12% of potassium, and 17% of selenium.

Chocolate Chips:
Buttery flavored cooking spray
1 ¼ cups powdered sugar
½ cup unsweetened cocoa powder
⅛ teaspoon salt
½ tablespoon fat-free margarine
3 ½ tablespoons skim milk
½ tablespoon vanilla extract

Dough:
Butter-flavored cooking spray
2 ¼ cups all-purpose flour
1 teaspoon baking soda

16

½ teaspoon salt
¼ cup fat-free margarine
¼ cup blackstrap molasses
¾ cup sugar
½ cup brown sugar
1 teaspoon vanilla extract
¼ cup fat-free egg substitute
1 ½ cups pine nuts

To make the chips, spray a pizza pan (or similar size pan) with cooking spray and wipe with a paper towel to spread evenly, absorbing the excess. Combine the sugar, cocoa, and salt in medium bowl. Add the remaining chocolate chip ingredients and mix until it makes a thick paste. Spread the paste on the pan until it's about ¼-inch thick. Put the pan, uncovered, in the refrigerator for about 2 hours. Then, using a non-serrated knife, make narrow (about ¼- to ½-inch thick) horizontal and vertical cuts so that the paste is cut into small cubes. Return the pan to the refrigerator and let sit, uncovered, for about 24 hours.

Preheat oven to 325°. Spray cookie sheets with cooking spray and wipe with a paper towel to spread evenly and absorb the excess.

In a medium bowl, combine the flour, baking soda, and salt. In a large bowl, combine the remaining dough ingredients, except the nuts. Add the dry to the wet and mix well. Add the nuts and mix well. Finally, use a spatula to remove the prepared chocolate chips from their pan and gently stir into the dough.

Drop large spoonfuls of completed dough onto the cookie sheets (about 2-3 tablespoons for each cookie) and bake for 11 minutes. Cool on the pan for 5 minutes. Use a spatula to remove from the pan and flip each cookie upside down onto foil. Cool completely.

The Basics	Power Punch	% Daily Value
Calories 351	Thiamin/B1 (0.3 mg)	22%
Protein 8 g	Iron (4.6 mg)	25%
Carbohydrate 61 g	Manganese (1.1 mg)	55%
Total fat 9 g		
% Calories from fat 23%		
Saturated fat 2 g		
Dietary Fiber 2 g		
Cholesterol 0 mg		
Sodium 282 mg		

Nutritional information per serving (based on12 servings; two large cookies per serving):

If you want to try my original fat-free version (that tastes even more like traditional chocolate chip cookies, but is not a Power Dessert), make the following changes to the previous recipe:

1) Omit the blackstrap molasses and add 2 tablespoons of light corn syrup.
2) Instead of ½ cup of brown sugar, add ¾ cup of brown sugar
3) Instead of 1 teaspoon of vanilla, add 2 teaspoons of vanilla
4) Omit the pine nuts

These changes will result in the following changes to the nutritional profile:

Calories = 267   % of calories from fat = 2%
Protein = 4 g   Saturated fat = 0 g
Total fat = 1 g   No "Power Punch"

Oatmeal Cranberry Cookies
Makes 24 Large Cookies

These are awesome cookies – a big hit with all of my taste-testers! In addition to the Power Punch nutrients listed below, each serving is a good source of the following (based on percent of Daily Values): 16% of fiber, 11% of thiamin/B1, 10% of riboflavin/B2, and 10% of iron.

Dough:
Butter-flavored cooking spray
2 cups quick oats
1 cup all-purpose flour
½ teaspoon baking soda
½ teaspoon salt
¼ cup fat-free margarine
1 ½ cups brown sugar
¼ cup maple syrup
¼ cup fat-free egg substitute
2 teaspoons vanilla extract
2 (6-ounce each) bags of dried, sweetened cranberries

Preheat oven to 325°. Spray cookie sheets with cooking spray and wipe with a paper towel to spread evenly and absorb the excess.

In a medium bowl, combine the oats, flour, baking soda, and salt. In a large bowl, combine the remaining dough ingredients, except the cranberries. Add the dry to the wet and mix well. Add the cranberries and mix well.

Drop large spoonfuls of dough onto the cookie sheets and bake for 20 minutes. Cool on the pan for 5 minutes. Then remove from pan.

19

Power Desserts

Nutritional information per serving (based on 12 servings; two large cookies per serving):

The Basics	Power Punch	% Daily Value
Calories 308	Manganese (0.9 mg)	48%
Protein 4 g	Cranberries (28 g)	
Carbohydrate 70 g		
Total fat 1 g		
% Calories from fat 4%		
Saturated fat 0 g		
Dietary Fiber 4 g		
Cholesterol 0 mg		
Sodium 203 mg		

Peanut Butter Brownies
Makes 18 Brownies

While my husband has had to suffer through many recipe failures, he also has the option to retain samples of recipes he loves rather than allowing them to circulate to other taste-testers. My Chief Recipe Tester exercised that option when I made these brownies! In addition to the Power Punch nutrients listed below, each serving is a good source of the following (based on percent of Daily Values): 12% of niacin/B3, 12% of vitamin D, and 11% of potassium.

Batter:
Butter-flavored cooking spray
Flour for dusting pan
1 (1-pound 6.5-ounce) box supreme brownie mix with chocolate syrup pouch
½ cup plain, nonfat yogurt
½ cup evaporated fat-free milk, canned
1⅓ cup instant skim milk powder
½ cup fat-free sweetened condensed milk

Filling:
1 ¼ cups reduced-fat creamy peanut butter
¼ cup evaporated fat-free milk, canned
3 tablespoons all-purpose flour
⅔ cup instant skim-milk powder
½ cup fat-free egg substitute
1 tablespoon vanilla extract
½ cup fat-free sweetened condensed milk

Frosting:
1 ¾ cups powdered sugar
3 tablespoons unsweetened cocoa powder
Pinch of salt
⅓ cup evaporated fat-free milk, canned

21

1 teaspoon vanilla extract

Preheat oven to 325°. Spray a 13x9-inch pan with cooking spray and wipe with a paper towel, to spread evenly and absorb the excess. Dust pan with flour until coated on bottom and sides. Discard excess flour.

Combine remaining batter ingredients and mix well. Spread evenly in pan. Combine filling ingredients and mix well. Spoon in thick vertical and horizontal stripes over the batter and swirl with a spoon or knife. Bake for 50 minutes.

Cool in pan for 10-15 minutes. Combine frosting ingredients. Spread evenly over brownies. Cool completely.

Nutritional information per serving (based on 18 servings):

The Basics	Power Punch	% Daily Value
Calories 392	Protein (12.6 g)	25%
Protein 13 g	Riboflavin/B2 (0.36 mg)	21%
Carbohydrate 65 g	Calcium (200 mg)	20%
Total fat 9 g	Phosphorus (211 mg)	21%
% Calories from fat 21%		
Saturated fat 2 g		
Dietary Fiber 2 g		
Cholesterol 3 mg		
Sodium 318 mg		

Chewy Maple Date Bars
Makes 12 Bars

My dad enjoyed these so much that he suggested that a batch would make a welcome Father's Day gift. What a great compliment – I'm happy to oblige! He also came up with the good idea of sprinkling powdered sugar on the bottom to prevent them from sticking after removing them from the pan. In addition to the Power Punch nutrients listed below, each serving is a good source of the following (based on percent of Daily Values): 12% of protein, 13% of niacin/B3, 11% of vitamin B6, 15% of folate, 16% of pantothenic acid, 13% of iron, 11% of magnesium, 19% of phosphorus, and 15% of potassium.

Ingredients:
Butter-flavored cooking spray
Flour for dusting pan
1 cup all-purpose flour
½ teaspoon baking powder
½ teaspoon cinnamon
¼ teaspoon salt
½ teaspoon maple flavoring
1 cup brown sugar
¾ cup fat-free egg substitute
2 teaspoons vanilla extract
2 (10-ounce each) packages chopped dates
1 ¼ cups salted sunflower seed kernels (make sure the kernels have no other added seasoning)
¼ cup maple syrup
Powdered sugar for dusting the bottom of the bars.

Preheat oven to 300°. Spray a 13x9-inch pan with cooking spray and wipe with a paper towel to spread evenly and absorb the excess. Dust pan with flour until coated on bottom and sides. Discard excess flour.

Combine the flour, baking powder, cinnamon, and salt in a medium bowl. In a large bowl, combine the maple flavoring, brown sugar, egg substitute, and vanilla. Add the dry to the wet and mix well. Stir in the dates.

Spread the batter evenly into the pan. Sprinkle the sunflower seed kernels over the batter. Drizzle the maple syrup over the kernels. Bake for 45 minutes. Cool in pan.

When removing the bars from the pan, turn them upside down and dust them with powdered sugar to prevent them from sticking.

Nutritional information per serving (based on 12 servings):

The Basics	Power Punch	% Daily Value
Calories 347	Dietary fiber (5.1 g)	20%
Protein 6 g	Riboflavin/B2 (0.35 mg)	20%
Carbohydrate 70 g	Vitamin E (10.4 IU)	35%
Total fat 7 g	Copper (0.5 mg)	23%
% Calories from fat 17%	Manganese (0.8 mg)	39%
Saturated fat 1 g	Selenium (15.3 mcg)	22%
Dietary Fiber 5 g		
Cholesterol 0 mg		
Sodium 213 mg		

Orange Snowballs
Makes 10 Servings

These tasty no-bake cookies combine the two great flavors of vanilla and tangy orange.

Ingredients:
1 (11 ounce) package of reduced-fat vanilla wafers
1 cup powdered sugar
½ cup frozen orange juice concentrate, thawed
1 tablespoon orange zest
Powdered sugar to coat cookies

Put vanilla wafers in a food processor to make crumbs. Combine crumbs, 1 cup powdered sugar, orange juice concentrate, and orange zest and mix well.

Shape into 1 ¼ to1 ½-inch diameter balls. Roll each in powdered sugar.

Nutritional information per serving (based on 10 servings; 3 cookies per serving):

The Basics	Power Punch	% Daily Value
Calories 206	Vitamin C (16 mg)	27%
Protein 1 g		
Carbohydrate 45 g		
Total fat 2 g		
% Calories from fat 10%		
Saturated fat 0 g		
Dietary Fiber 0 g		
Cholesterol 0 mg		
Sodium 114 mg		

25

Amaretto Cheesecake Brownies
Makes 18 Brownies

I made these brownies for a dinner party hosted by my friend Eileen on behalf of our friend and boss Lori's birthday. They were a big hit – an altogether new way to score "brownie points" with the boss! In addition to the Power Punch nutrients listed below, each serving is a good source of the following (based on percent of Daily Values): 18% of protein, 11% of fiber, 14% of riboflavin/B2, 12% of calcium, 11% of iron, 12% of magnesium, and 17% of phosphorus.

Batter:
Butter-flavored cooking spray
Flour for dusting pan
1 (1-pound 6.5-ounce) box supreme brownie mix with chocolate syrup pouch
½ cup plain, nonfat yogurt
½ cup evaporated fat-free milk, canned

Filling:
1 (8 ounce) package of fat-free cream cheese
7 ounces almond paste
1 tablespoon cornstarch
1 tablespoon Amaretto liqueur
½ teaspoon almond extract
¼ cup fat-free egg substitute

Frosting:
2 cups powdered sugar
3 tablespoons unsweetened cocoa powder
Pinch of salt
⅓ cup evaporated fat-free milk, canned
1 teaspoon vanilla extract
½ teaspoon almond extract

1 ¼ cups almond slices

Preheat oven to 325°. Spray a 13x9-pan with cooking spray and wipe with a paper towel to spread evenly and absorb the excess. Dust pan with flour until coated on bottom and sides. Discard excess flour.

Combine remaining batter ingredients and mix well. Spread evenly in pan. Combine filling ingredients and mix well. Spoon in thick vertical and horizontal stripes over the batter and swirl with a spoon or knife. Bake for 50 minutes.

Cool in pan for 10-15 minutes. Combine all frosting ingredients, except almonds. Spread frosting evenly over brownies. Toast the almonds, and sprinkle over the icing. Cool completely.

Nutritional information per serving (based on 18 servings):

The Basics	Power Punch	% Daily Value
Calories 362	Vitamin E 6.2 IU	21%
Protein 9 g		
Carbohydrate 51 g		
Total fat 14 g		
% Calories from fat 34%		
Saturated fat 2 g		
Dietary Fiber 3 g		
Cholesterol 2 mg		
Sodium 206 mg		

Pineapple Walnut Bars
Makes 9 Bars

The sweetened condensed milk caramelizes the walnuts as they bake – a great contrast with the moist pineapple. In addition to the Power Punch nutrients listed below, each serving is a good source of the following (based on percent of Daily Values): 16% of protein, 11% of thiamin/B1, 16% of riboflavin/B2, 15% of calcium, 17% of copper, 12% of magnesium, and 19% of phosphorus.

Ingredients:
Butter-flavored cooking spray
1 ½ cups graham cracker crumbs
1 (20 ounce) can crushed pineapple, in its own juice
1 (14 ounce) can fat-free sweetened condensed milk
1 ⅓ cups chopped walnuts

Preheat oven to 325°. Spray an 8 ½-inch square pan with cooking spray and wipe with a paper towel to spread evenly and absorb the excess.

Sprinkle the graham cracker crumbs evenly over the bottom of the pan. Drizzle the juice from the pineapple over the crumbs. Then drizzle almost half of the condensed milk over the crumbs.

Spoon the crushed pineapple on top of the crumbs evenly. Sprinkle the walnuts over the pineapple. Drizzle the remaining condensed milk over the walnuts.

Bake for 55 minutes. Cool completely.

Nutritional information per serving (based on 9 servings):

The Basics	Power Punch	% Daily Value
Calories 367	Manganese (0.8 mg)	40%
Protein 8 g	Omega 3 fatty acids (1.8 g)	
Carbohydrate 53 g	Omega 6 fatty acids (7.9 g)	
Total fat 14 g		
% Calories from fat 35%		
Saturated fat 1 g		
Dietary Fiber 2 g		
Cholesterol 3 mg		
Sodium 173 mg		

Oatmeal Raisin Cookies
Makes 24 Cookies

These are so easy to make because they start with cookie mix. In addition to the Power Punch nutrients listed below, each serving is a good source of fiber (10%) based on percent of Daily Values.

Batter:
1 ½ cups raisins
⅔ cup carrot juice, canned
1 (17.5 ounce) pouch of oatmeal cookie mix (with no raisins)
½ cup solid pack pumpkin, canned
2 tablespoons light corn syrup

Soak the raisins in the carrot juice in the refrigerator, uncovered, for about two hours, stirring once or twice.

Preheat oven to 350°. Combine the remaining ingredients with the excess carrot juice from the bowl of raisins and mix well. Then stir in the raisins.

Drop by rounded tablespoonfuls onto ungreased cookie sheets. Bake for 15 minutes. Cool completely. Makes 24 cookies.

Nutritional information per serving (based on 12 servings; two cookies per serving):

The Basics	Power Punch	% Daily Value
Calories 264	Vitamin A (2950 IU)	59%
Protein 4 g	Manganese (0.6 mg)	29%
Carbohydrate 47 g		
Total fat 8 g		
% Calories from fat 26%		
Saturated fat 2 g		
Dietary Fiber 2 g		
Cholesterol 0 mg		
Sodium 206 mg		

Sunflower Macaroons
Makes 36 Cookies

These are fast, easy, and delicious! In addition to the
Power Punch nutrients listed below, each serving is a good
source of the following (based on percent of Daily Values):
16% of protein, 11% of riboflavin/B2, 13% of folate, 16% of
pantothenic acid, and 10% of calcium.

Ingredients:
Butter-flavored cooking spray
¼ cup fat-free egg substitute
1 (14 ounce) can fat-free sweetened condensed milk
1 teaspoon coconut extract
1 teaspoon vanilla extract
1 (14.5 ounce) box of angel food cake mix
¼ cup flaked, sweetened coconut
3 cups salted sunflower seed kernels (make sure the kernels
    have no other added seasoning)

Preheat oven to 350°. Spray cookie sheets with cooking
spray and wipe with a paper towel to spread evenly and
absorb the excess.

Combine the egg substitute, condensed milk, and extracts
in a large bowl and mix well. Add the cake mix, and mix
well. Then stir in the coconut and sunflower kernels.

Drop by rounded spoonfuls onto cookie sheets. Bake for 10
minutes. Cool a few minutes on the pan before removing.

Nutritional information per serving (based on 18 servings; two cookies per serving):

The Basics	Power Punch	% Daily Value
Calories 278	Vitamin E (16.1 IU)	54%
Protein 8 g	Copper (0.4 mg)	20%
Carbohydrate 38 g	Manganese (0.5 mg)	24%
Total fat 11 g	Phosphorus (298 mg)	30%
% Calories from fat 35%	Selenium (17.1 mcg)	24%
Saturated fat 1 g	Omega-6 fatty acids (7 g)	
Dietary Fiber 2 g		
Cholesterol 1 mg		
Sodium 397 mg		

Chocolate Peanut Butter Crunch Bars
Makes 15 Bars

This easy recipe requires no cooking or baking. These crispy-chewy bars are very rich-tasting. By taste alone, you'd never guess they had pumpkin seed kernels in them (which add a lot of the nutrients). In addition to the Power Punch nutrients listed below, each serving is a good source of the following (based on percent of Daily Values): 10% of fiber, 15% of thiamin/B1, 12% of vitamin B6, 10% of vitamin C, 13% of folate, 16% of calcium, 17% of potassium, and 14% of zinc.

Bars:
Butter-flavored cooking spray
1 (14 ounce) can fat-free sweetened condensed milk
¼ cup blackstrap molasses
1 cup reduced-fat creamy peanut butter
1 teaspoon vanilla extract
6 cups crisp rice cereal
1 ½ cups pumpkin seed kernels

Icing:
2 cups powdered sugar
4 tablespoons unsweetened cocoa powder
Pinch of salt
⅓ cup of evaporated fat-free milk, canned
1 teaspoon vanilla extract

Spray a 13x9-inch pan with cooking spray and wipe with a paper towel to spread evenly and absorb the excess.

Combine all of the bar ingredients, except the cereal and kernels, in a large bowl. Then stir in the cereal and kernels. Spread into pan.

Combine all icing ingredients and spread over the bars.

Nutritional information per serving (based on 15 servings):

The Basics	Power Punch	% Daily Value
Calories 405	Protein (15.9 g)	32%
Protein 16 g	Riboflavin/B2 (0.35 mg)	21%
Carbohydrate 54 g	Niacin/B3 (4.5 mg)	22%
Total fat 16 g	Copper (0.45 mg)	23%
% Calories from fat 33%	Iron (5.5 mg)	31%
Saturated fat 3 g	Magnesium (145 mg)	36%
Dietary Fiber 2 g	Manganese (0.94 mg)	47%
Cholesterol 2 mg	Phosphorus (417 mg)	42%
Sodium 386 mg		

Strawberries & Cream Bars
Makes 12 Bars

This refreshing, delicious dessert was inspired by a recipe given to me by my sister Lauren. It starts with a sweet crust made with pretzels and is topped with a creamy strawberry layer. You can reduce the sodium content to under 300 mg per serving by using unsalted pretzels. In addition to the Power Punch nutrients listed below, each serving is a good source of the following (based on percent of Daily Values): 18% of protein, 15% of vitamin A, 10% of folate, and 14% of calcium.

Crust:
2 cups finely crushed pretzel crumbs
2 cups powdered sugar
¼ cup fat-free margarine
¼ cup plain, nonfat yogurt

Strawberry Layer:
2 (4-serving) packages strawberry Jello® mix
1 ½ cups boiling water
16 ounces soft, fat-free cream cheese
1 cup fat-free frozen whipped topping, thawed
2 (16-ounce each) bags unsweetened, frozen, whole strawberries, thawed

To make crust, combine pretzel crumbs and powdered sugar. Add margarine and yogurt and mix until crumbs are evenly moistened. Press into a 13 x 9" pan. In a large bowl, combine Jello® and boiling water. Stir about two minutes, or until mix is dissolved. In a medium bowl, combine the cream cheese and whipped topping and mix well. Add the cream cheese mixture to the Jello® mixture

36

and mix well. Refrigerate for about 45 minutes. Stir in the strawberries. Pour the strawberry mixture over the crust and refrigerate until set.

Nutritional information per serving (based on 12 servings):

The Basics		Power Punch	% Daily Value
Calories	263	Riboflavin/B2 (0.51 mg)	30%
Protein	9 g	Vitamin C (31 mg)	52%
Carbohydrate	56 g	Manganese (0.5 mg)	25%
Total fat	1 g	Phosphorus (200 mg)	20%
Calories from fat	2%	Strawberries (76 g)	
Saturated fat	0 g		
Dietary Fiber	2 g		
Cholesterol	3mg		
Sodium	519 g		

Power Desserts

Cakes

Hazelnut Fudge Cake
Makes 1 Cake (16 Servings)

This is a beautiful and fabulously rich-tasting cake with a moist fudge center that forms during baking – a chocolate lover's dream! In addition to the Power Punch nutrients listed below, each serving is a good source of the following (based on percent of Daily Values): 18% of protein, 15% of fiber, 17% of thiamin (B1), 15% of vitamin E, 14% of folate, 14% of calcium, 11% of magnesium, 12% of phosphorus, 14% of potassium, and 11% of selenium.

Batter:
Butter-flavored cooking spray
Flour for dusting pan
2 ¼ cups all-purpose flour
2 cups powdered sugar
¾ cup unsweetened cocoa powder
1 teaspoon salt
1 ¾ cups sugar
1 cup fat-free egg substitute
1 (12 ounce) can evaporated fat-free milk (reserving 3 tablespoons for the icing)
2 teaspoons vanilla extract
¼ cup blackstrap molasses
2 cups chopped hazelnuts

Icing:
¾ cup powdered sugar
¼ cup unsweetened cocoa powder
Pinch of salt
1 teaspoon vanilla extract
The reserved evaporated fat-free milk
½ cup chopped hazelnuts

Preheat oven to 325°. Spray Bundt® or tube pan with cooking spray and wipe with a paper towel to spread evenly and absorb the excess. Dust pan with flour until coated on bottom and sides. Discard excess flour. It is very important to thoroughly oil and flour the pan for this recipe to prevent the cake from sticking to the pan.

For the batter, combine the flour, powdered sugar, cocoa, and salt in a small bowl. In a large bowl, combine sugar, egg substitute, evaporated milk (make sure you reserve 3 tablespoons for the icing), vanilla, and molasses. Mix well. Add the dry ingredients to the wet and mix well. Stir in the hazelnuts.

Pour batter into the pan and bake for 1 hour. Be sure not to over-bake this cake. The toothpick test will not work for this recipe as the center should remain fudgy. Cool in pan for 1 hour. Loosen the sides of the cake and carefully remove from the pan. Combine all icing ingredients, except hazelnuts, and drizzle over cake. Toast hazelnuts and press into icing around the top of the cake.

Nutritional information per serving (based on 16 servings):

The Basics	Power Punch	% Daily Value
Calories 403	Riboflavin/B2 (0.4 mg)	24%
Protein 9 g	Copper (0.46 mg)	23%
Carbohydrate 68 g	Iron (3.54 mg)	20%
Total fat 12 g	Manganese (1.37 mg)	68%
% Calories from fat 25%		
Saturated fat 1 g		
Dietary Fiber 4 g		
Cholesterol 0 mg		
Sodium 229 mg		

Blueberries & Cream Cake
Makes 1 Cake (12 Servings)

This easy cake has a lightly spiced sour cream icing. In addition to the Power Punch nutrients listed below, each serving is a good source of the following (based on percent of Daily Values): 18% of protein, 10% of fiber, 15% of thiamin (B1), 10% of vitamin E, 10% of folate, 10% of magnesium, 10% of manganese, and 11% of selenium.

Batter:
Butter-flavored cooking spray
2 cups all-purpose flour
1 teaspoon baking powder
1 teaspoon cinnamon
½ teaspoon salt
½ cup sugar
1 (14 ounce) can fat-free sweetened condensed milk
¼ cup fat-free egg substitute
1 tablespoon vanilla extract
½ cup fat-free sour cream from a 16 ounce container (reserving the rest for the icing)
1 (16 ounce) bag of frozen blueberries (unsweetened), thawed

Icing:
Remaining sour cream
⅔ cup powdered sugar
½ teaspoon vanilla extract
¼ teaspoon cinnamon
¼ teaspoon nutmeg
1 cup sliced almonds

Preheat oven to 325°. Spray a 13x9-inch pan with cooking spray and wipe with a paper towel to spread evenly and absorb the excess.

Combine the flour, baking powder, cinnamon, and salt in a medium bowl. In a large bowl, combine the sugar, condensed milk, egg substitute, vanilla, and sour cream. Add the dry to the wet and mix well. Gently stir in thawed blueberries. Pour into the pan and bake for 1 hour. Combine all icing ingredients, except almonds, and spread over warm cake. Toast the almonds and sprinkle over the icing. Cool completely.

Nutritional information per serving (based on 12 servings):

The Basics	Power Punch	% Daily Value
Calories 335	Riboflavin/B2 (0.47 mg)	27%
Protein 9 g	Calcium (200 mg)	20%
Carbohydrate 63 g	Phosphorus (198 mg)	20%
Total fat 5 g	Blueberries (38 g)	
% Calories from fat 13%		
Saturated fat 1 g		
Dietary Fiber 3 g		
Cholesterol 6 mg		
Sodium 211 mg		

Banana Walnut Pudding Cake
Makes 1 Cake (14 Servings)

This pretty cake is wonderfully moist thanks to the pudding and sour cream. My friend Annette loved it so much that she claimed it as her birthday cake of choice! In addition to the Power Punch nutrients listed below, each serving is a good source of the following (based on percent of Daily Values): 14% of protein, 11% of thiamin (B1), 10% of riboflavin (B2), 12% of vitamin B6, 13% of calcium, and 11% copper.

Batter:
Butter-flavored cooking spray
Flour for pans
1 cup very ripe bananas, mashed (about 2 medium bananas)
1 (18.25 ounce) package spice cake mix
1 (3.4 ounce) package instant banana cream pudding mix
1 cup nonfat sour cream
1 (12 ounce) can evaporated fat-free milk
1 ⅓ cup walnuts, chopped

Filling/Frosting:
1 (12 ounce) container fat-free frozen whipped topping, thawed
1 cup very ripe bananas, mashed (about 2 medium bananas)
1 (3.4 ounce) package instant banana cream pudding mix

Preheat oven to 300°. Spray three 8 ½ -inch round pans with cooking spray and wipe with a paper towel to spread evenly and absorb the excess. Dust pans with flour until coated on bottom and sides. Discard excess flour.

Combine all remaining batter ingredients, except walnuts, and mix well. Stir in walnuts. Spread batter evenly in the three pans. Bake for 1 hour and 10 minutes. Cool completely in pans. Then remove cake layers from pans by loosening the sides and turning them upside down onto wax paper.

Combine all filling/frosting ingredients and mix well. Assemble cake, spreading filling/frosting between layers, on top, and on sides of cake.

Nutritional information per serving (based on 14 servings):

The Basics	Power Punch	% Daily Value
Calories 393	Manganese (0.44 mg)	22%
Protein 7 g	Omega-3 fatty acids (1 g)	
Carbohydrate 64 g	Omega-6 fatty acids (4.4 g)	
Total fat 12 g		
% Calories from fat 28%		
Saturated fat 2 g		
Dietary Fiber 2 g		
Cholesterol 12 mg		
Sodium 537 mg		

Loads-of-Carrot Cake
Makes 1 Cake (12 Servings)

This cake has significantly more carrots than most carrot cakes, plus the added nutrients of carrot juice. It is topped with a sweet, cream-cheese icing. In addition to the Power Punch nutrients listed below, each serving is a good source of the following (based on percent of Daily Values): 13% of protein, 11% of fiber, 12% of thiamin/B1, 12% of calcium, 11% of iron, 10% of manganese, and 14% of phosphorus.

Batter:
Butter-flavored cooking spray
1 (16 ounce) bag ready-to-eat baby carrots
1 cup all-purpose flour
1 cup whole wheat flour
1 teaspoon baking powder
1 teaspoon baking soda
2 tablespoons cornstarch
2 teaspoons cinnamon
½ teaspoon ginger
½ teaspoon nutmeg
½ teaspoon salt
1 cup brown sugar
1 cup sugar
¼ cup fat-free egg substitute
1 (12 ounce) can of carrot juice
2 teaspoons vanilla

Icing:
1 (8 ounce) tub soft, fat-free cream cheese
2 cups powdered sugar
1 teaspoon vanilla extract

46

Preheat oven to 325°. Spray a 13x9-inch pan with cooking spray and wipe with a paper towel to spread evenly and absorb the excess.

Put the carrots in a food processor and shred into small pieces. Combine the flours, baking powder, baking soda, cornstarch, spices, and salt in a medium bowl. In a large bowl, combine the sugars, egg substitute, carrot juice, and vanilla. Add the dry to the wet and mix well. Stir in the processed carrots. Pour into the pan and bake for 1 hour. Cool completely.

Combine all icing ingredients and mix well. Spread over cake.

Nutritional information per serving (based on 12 servings):

The Basics	Power Punch	% Daily Value
Calories 345	Vitamin A (9216 IU)	184%
Protein 7 g	Riboflavin/B2 (0.37 mg)	22%
Carbohydrate 79 g	Carrots/carrot juice (67 g)	
Total fat 1 g		
% Calories from fat 2%		
Saturated fat 0 g		
Dietary Fiber 3 g		
Cholesterol 1 mg		
Sodium 374 mg		

German Chocolate Cake
Makes 1 Cake (14 Servings)

This classic beauty was loved by all who tasted it. In addition to the Power Punch nutrients listed below, each serving is a good source of the following (based on percent of Daily Values): 19% of protein, 15% of thiamin (B1), 15% of vitamin D, 10% of iron, 12% of potassium, and 12% of selenium.

Batter:
Butter-flavored cooking spray
2 cups all-purpose flour
¼ cup powdered sugar
1 teaspoon baking soda
½ teaspoon salt
½ cup unsweetened cocoa powder
1 cup instant skim milk powder
2 cups sugar
1 teaspoon vanilla
½ cup plain, nonfat yogurt
½ cup fat-free egg substitute
¾ cup evaporated fat-free milk, canned

Icing:
1 (3.4 ounce) package instant coconut cream pudding mix
1 (3.4 ounce) package instant vanilla pudding mix
½ cup brown sugar
1 tablespoon praline/pecan liqueur
2 cups evaporated fat-free milk, canned
1 cup chopped pecans

Preheat oven to 325°. Spray three 8 ½ -inch round pans with cooking spray and wipe with a paper towel to spread evenly and absorb the excess.

48

Combine flour, powdered sugar, baking soda, salt, cocoa, and milk powder in a medium bowl. Combine remaining-batter ingredients in a large bowl and mix well. Add the dry to the wet and mix well. Pour the batter evenly into the three pans. Bake for 35 minutes. Cool for 5 minutes in pans. Then remove cake layers from pans by loosening the sides and turning them upside down onto wax paper. Cool completely.

Toast the pecans and let cool; chop them into small pieces. Combine all filling/frosting ingredients, except pecans, and mix well. Stir in the pecans. Put the mixture in the refrigerator, uncovered, until thick enough to spread. Assemble cake, spreading filling/frosting between layers, on top, and on sides of cake.

Nutritional information per serving (based on 14 servings):

The Basics	Power Punch	% Daily Value
Calories 405	Riboflavin/B2 (0.47 mg)	28%
Protein 9 g	Calcium (221 mg)	22%
Carbohydrate 77 g	Manganese (0.54 mg)	27%
Total fat 7 g	Phosphorus (286 mg)	29%
% Calories from fat 15%		
Saturated fat 1 g		
Dietary Fiber 2 g		
Cholesterol 1 mg		
Sodium 471 mg		

Iced Almond Pound Cake
Makes 1 Cake (16 Servings)

The cinnamon-almond filling in the center of this cake makes it taste extra rich and delicious. Almond butter, used in the batter, is carried by most grocery stores. Look for it near the peanut butter or in the health food section. In addition to the Power Punch nutrients listed below, each serving is a good source of the following (based on percent of Daily Values): 16% of protein, 11% of thiamin (B1), 10% of folate, 15% of calcium, 15% of copper, and 11% of iron.

Filling:
½ cup light brown sugar
⅓ cup quick oats
1 teaspoon cinnamon
2 tablespoons fat-free margarine
1 cup chopped almonds

Batter:
Butter-flavored cooking spray
Powdered sugar for dusting pan
2 cups all-purpose flour
1 teaspoon baking powder
1 teaspoon salt
1 cup sugar
1 cup almond butter
¼ cup fat-free egg substitute
1 teaspoon almond extract
1 teaspoon vanilla extract
1 ¼ cup evaporated fat-free milk, canned

Icing:
1 cup powdered sugar
½ teaspoon almond extract

50

2 tablespoons evaporated fat-free milk, canned

Preheat oven to 325°. Spray Bundt® or tube pan with cooking spray and wipe with a paper towel to spread evenly and absorb the excess. Dust pan with sugar until coated on bottom and sides. Discard excess sugar.

Toast the almonds. After they have cooled, chop into very small pieces (a food processor is the easiest way to do this). Combine all filling ingredients in a bowl and stir until evenly moistened. Set aside.

Combine the flour, baking powder, and salt in a small bowl. In a larger bowl, combine remaining batter ingredients and mix well. Add the dry ingredients to the wet and mix well.
Pour half of the batter into the pan. Spoon the filling in a ring around the center of the batter, being careful so that the filling does not touch the sides of the pan. Gently press the filling part-way into the batter. Cover the filling with remaining batter. Bake for 55 minutes. Cool 15 minutes, then remove from pan. Combine icing ingredients and drizzle over cake.

Nutritional information per serving (based on 16 servings):

The Basics	Power Punch	% Daily Value
Calories 341	Riboflavin/B2 (0.36 mg)	21%
Protein 8 g	Vitamin E (7.48 IU)	25%
Carbohydrate 48 g	Magnesium (82 mg)	20%
Total fat 14 g	Manganese (0.58 mg)	29%
% Calories from fat 36%	Phosphorus (203 mg)	20%
Saturated fat 1 g		
Dietary Fiber 2 g		
Cholesterol 0 mg		
Sodium 228 mg		

Kahlua & Cream Cake
Makes 1 Cake (8 Servings)

This delicious fat-free cake has an attractive speckled icing. If you prefer mocha flavor, use chocolate pudding mix instead of vanilla. In addition to the Power Punch nutrients listed below, each serving is a good source of the following (based on percent of Daily Values): 10% of thiamin (B1), 12% of vitamin D, and 10% of selenium.

Batter:
Butter-flavored cooking spray
1 cup all-purpose flour
1 teaspoon baking powder
¼ teaspoon salt
1 cup sugar
½ cup fat-free egg substitute
½ cup evaporated fat-free milk, canned
1 tablespoon Kahlua liqueur

Filling:
1 (3.4 ounce) package instant vanilla pudding mix
1 cup evaporated fat-free milk, canned
1 tablespoon Kahlua liqueur

Icing:
1 ½ cup powdered sugar
Pinch of salt
1 teaspoon instant coffee powder
3-4 tablespoons evaporated fat-free milk, canned
1 teaspoon vanilla extract

Preheat oven to 325°. Spray one 8 ½ -inch round pan with cooking spray and wipe with a paper towel to spread evenly and absorb the excess.

Combine the flour, baking powder, and salt in a medium bowl. In a large bowl, combine the remaining batter ingredients. Add the dry mixture to the wet mixture and mix well. Pour into the pan and bake for 35 minutes. Cool for 5 minutes before removing the cake from the pan. Then cool completely.

Slice the cake in half horizontally with a long knife so that there are two layers. Combine the filling ingredients and spread between the two layers. Combine the icing ingredients and pour evenly over the top and sides of the cake.

Nutritional information per serving (based on 8 servings):

The Basics	Power Punch	% Daily Value
Calories 351	Calcium (203 mg)	20%
Protein 7 g	Phosphorus (223 mg)	22%
Carbohydrate 79 g	Riboflavin/B2 (0.47 mg)	28%
Total fat 0 g		
% Calories from fat 1%		
Saturated fat 0 g		
Dietary Fiber 0 g		
Cholesterol 2 mg		
Sodium 439 mg		

Zucchini Date Cake
Makes 1 Cake (12 Servings)

If you like zucchini bread, you'll love this cake. The dates give it an extra rich taste. In addition to the Power Punch nutrients listed below, each serving is a good source of the following (based on percent of Daily Values): 16% of protein, 14% of thiamin (B1), 16% of riboflavin (B2), 11% of niacin (B3), 10% of folate, 12% of calcium, 10% of copper, 14% of iron, 15% of manganese, and 12% of potassium.

Batter:
Butter-flavored cooking spray
2 cups whole wheat flour
¾ cup all-purpose flour
1 teaspoon baking powder
1 teaspoon baking soda
1 teaspoon cinnamon
½ teaspoon salt
1 ½ cups brown sugar
½ cup fat-free egg substitute
1 teaspoon vanilla extract
½ teaspoon coconut extract
1 cup plain, nonfat yogurt
4 cups grated zucchini
1 (10 ounce) container chopped dates
¼ cup sweetened, flaked coconut

Icing:
1 (8 ounce) container non-fat sour cream
2 cups powdered sugar
½ teaspoon vanilla extract
¼ teaspoon cinnamon

Preheat oven to 325°. Spray a 13x9-inch pan with cooking spray and wipe with a paper towel to spread evenly and absorb the excess.

Combine the flours, baking powder, baking soda, cinnamon, and salt in a medium bowl. In a large bowl, combine the sugar, egg substitute, extracts, and yogurt. Add the dry to the wet and mix well. Stir in the zucchini, coconut and dates. Pour into the pan and bake for 1 hour. Allow the cake to cool. Combine all icing ingredients and spread over cake.

Nutritional information per serving (based on 12 servings):

The Basics	Power Punch	% Daily Value
Calories 402	Dietary fiber (5.35 g)	21%
Protein 8 g	Zucchini (43 g)	
Carbohydrate 92 g		
Total fat 2 g		
% Calories from fat 4		
Saturated fat 1 g		
Dietary Fiber 5 g		
Cholesterol 2 mg		
Sodium 305 mg		

Cream Cheese Pound Cake
Makes 1 Loaf Cake (10 Slices)

This mellow cake can be eaten plain or spruced up with fresh strawberries and chocolate syrup. The nutritional information provided is for a plain serving. In addition to the Power Punch nutrients listed below, each serving is a good source of the following (based on percent of Daily Values): 19% of vitamin A, 16% of thiamin (B1), 13% of folate, and 12% of selenium.

Batter:
Butter-flavored cooking spray
2 cups all-purpose flour
1 cup powdered sugar
½ teaspoon baking powder
2 (8-ounce each) packages fat free cream cheese
1 (14 ounce) can fat-free sweetened condensed milk
1 cup fat-free egg substitute
1 teaspoon vanilla extract
1 teaspoon lemon extract

Preheat oven to 300°. Spray a loaf pan with cooking spray and wipe with a paper towel to spread evenly and absorb the excess.

Combine the flour, powdered sugar, and baking powder in a medium bowl. In a large bowl, combine the remaining batter ingredients. Add the dry to the wet and mix well. Pour into the pan and bake for 2 hours. Cool for about 2 hours, then remove from the pan.

Power Desserts

Nutritional information per serving (based on 10 servings):

The Basics	Power Punch	% Daily Value
Calories 303	Protein (15 g)	30%
Protein 15 g	Riboflavin/B2 (0.74 mg)	44%
Carbohydrate 59 g	Calcium (266 mg)	27%
Total fat 0 g	Phosphorus (286 mg)	29%
% Calories from fat 1		
Saturated fat 0 g		
Dietary Fiber 1 g		
Cholesterol 7 mg		
Sodium 335 mg		

Tropical Cake
Makes 1 Cake (12 Servings)

This cake is as easy as opening a box and a few cans; and it has a great blend of tropical flavors. In addition to the Power Punch nutrients listed below, each serving is a good source of riboflavin/B2 (10%).

Batter:
Butter-flavored cooking spray
1 (18.25 ounce) package yellow cake mix
1 (12 ounce) can carrot juice
½ cup fat-free egg substitute
1 (20 ounce) can crushed pineapple, in its own juice (divided)
½ cup chopped macadamia nuts

Icing:
¾ cup powdered sugar
2 tablespoons of the reserved pineapple juice
The reserved pineapple
¼ cup sweetened, flaked coconut

Preheat oven to 350°. Spray a 13x9-inch pan with cooking spray and wipe with a paper towel to spread evenly and absorb the excess.

Combine the cake mix, carrot juice, and egg substitute in a large bowl. Drain pineapple, but reserve 2 tablespoons juice for icing. Add 1 cup of pineapple to the batter, and reserve the rest. Stir the pineapple into batter and pour into pan. Sprinkle the nuts over the batter. Bake for 40 minutes. Cool for 15 minutes.

Combine powdered sugar, reserved pineapple juice and remaining reserved pineapple. Spread evenly over cake. Toast coconut and sprinkle over cake.

Nutritional information per serving (based on 12 servings):

The Basics	Power Punch	% Daily Value
Calories 291	Vitamin A (3279 IU)	66%
Protein 3 g	Carrot juice (29 g)	
Carbohydrate 53 g		
Total fat 8 g		
% Calories from fat 23		
Saturated fat 2 g		
Dietary Fiber 1 g		
Cholesterol 0 mg		
Sodium 327 mg		

Power Desserts

Pies

Chocolate Peanut Butter Pie
Makes 1 Pie (8 Slices)

This is a very decadent, delicious pie made with the classic chocolate – peanut butter combo. In addition to the Power Punch nutrients listed below, each serving is a good source of the following (based on percent of Daily Values): 11% of fiber, 16% of vitamin D, 11% of iron, 10% of vitamin A, and 15% of potassium.

Crust:
Butter-flavored cooking spray
12 reduced-fat Oreo cookies
¼ cup instant skim milk powder
¼ cup powdered sugar
2 tablespoons fat-free margarine

Filling:
1 cup sugar
1 cup reduced-fat peanut butter
1 tablespoon cornstarch
1 teaspoon vanilla extract
¼ cup egg substitute
½ cup evaporated fat-free milk, canned
1 cup instant skim milk powder

Icing:
½ cup powdered sugar
2 tablespoons unsweetened cocoa powder
Pinch of salt
2 tablespoons canned, evaporated fat-free milk
¼ teaspoon vanilla extract

Preheat oven to 325°. Spray a pie pan with cooking spray and wipe with a paper towel to spread evenly and absorb the excess.

Use a food processor to make crumbs from the cookies. Combine the cookie crumbs, milk powder, and powdered sugar in a bowl. Then add margarine and mix until crumbs are evenly moistened. Press them into the bottom and part-way up the sides of the pan.

Combine all of the filling ingredients and mix well. Pour into pie crust and bake for 35-40 minutes. Allow the pie to cool for one hour.

Combine the icing ingredients and spread evenly over the pie.

Nutritional information per serving (based on 8 servings):

The Basics	Power Punch	% Daily Value
Calories 439	Protein (15.9 g)	32%
Protein 16 g	Riboflavin/B2 (0.35 mg)	21%
Carbohydrate 69 g	Niacin/B3 (4.26 mg)	21%
Total fat13 g	Calcium (198 mg)	20%
Calories from fat 25%	Phosporus (261 mg)	26%
Saturated fat 3 g		
Dietary Fiber 3 g		
Cholesterol 2 mg		
Sodium 318 mg		

Raspberry Lemon Pie
Makes 1 Pie (8 Slices)

This is a refreshingly sweet and tangy pie. In addition to the Power Punch nutrients listed below, each serving is a good source of the following (based on percent of Daily Values): 15% of protein, 14% of fiber, 16% of calcium, and 14% of phosphorus.

Crust:
Butter-flavored cooking spray
1 ¼ cups graham cracker crumbs
¼ cup sugar
2 tablespoons fat-free margarine

Filling:
1 (14 ounce) can fat-free sweetened condensed milk
½ cup egg substitute
½ cup lemon juice

Topping:
1 (12 ounce) bag of frozen raspberries, thawed
⅓ cup sugar

Preheat oven to 325°. Spray a pie pan with cooking spray and wipe with a paper towel to spread evenly and absorb the excess.

Combine the crumbs, sugar and margarine, and mix until crumbs are evenly moistened. Press them into the bottom and part-way up the sides of the pan.

Combine the filling ingredients and mix well. Pour into pie crust and bake for 45 minutes.

While the pie is cooling, gently stir the sugar into the raspberries. Let sit until the sugar has dissolved, stirring occasionally. When pie is completely cooled, spoon the topping evenly over the pie.

Nutritional information per serving (based on 8 servings):

The Basics	Power Punch	% Daily Value
Calories 307	Riboflavin/B2 (0.5 mg)	31%
Protein 8 g	Vitamin C (18 mg)	30%
Carbohydrate 65 g	Manganese (0.6 mg)	29%
Total fat 2 g	Raspberries (43 g)	
% Calories from fat 6		
Saturated fat 0 g		
Dietary Fiber 3 g		
Cholesterol 3 mg		
Sodium 220 mg		

Candied Sweet Potato Pie
Makes 1 Pie (8 Slices)

The flavors of orange, maple, and coconut blend together sweetly in this variation on a southern classic. In addition to the Power Punch nutrients listed below, each serving is a good source of the following (based on percent of Daily Values): 11% of fiber, 15% of riboflavin/B2, and 10% of iron.

Crust:
Butter-flavored cooking spray
1 ¼ cups graham cracker crumbs
¼ cup sugar
2 tablespoons fat-free margarine
¼ teaspoon maple extract
¼ teaspoon coconut extract

Filling:
1 (29 ounce) can of yams/sweet potatoes in syrup
¼ cup egg substitute
¼ cup sugar
⅓ cup orange marmalade
½ teaspoon cinnamon
½ teaspoon ginger
½ teaspoon salt
½ cup canned, evaporated fat-free milk
1 teaspoon vanilla
¼ cup maple syrup
2 tablespoons sweetened, flaked coconut
½ tablespoon cornstarch

Preheat oven to 325°. Spray a pie pan with cooking spray and wipe with a paper towel to spread evenly and absorb the excess.

66

Power Desserts

Combine the crumbs, sugar, margarine and extracts, and mix until crumbs are evenly moistened. Press them into the bottom and part-way up the sides of the pan.

Drain the liquid from the can of sweet potatoes or yams and mash the potatoes in a large bowl. Add the remaining filling-ingredients and mix well. Pour into pie crust and bake for 1 hour.

Nutritional information per serving (based on 8 servings):

The Basics	Power Punch	% Daily Value
Calories 292	Vitamin A (5372 IU)	107%
Protein 4 g	Manganese (1.0 mg)	48%
Carbohydrate 64 g	Sweet potatoes (72 g)	
Total fat 3 g		
% Calories from fat 8		
Saturated fat 1 g		
Dietary Fiber 3 g		
Cholesterol 0 mg		
Sodium 356 mg		

Maple Walnut Pie
Makes 1 Pie (8 Slices)

This is one of my favorite pies, and a sweet way to get a good dose of those healthy Omega fatty acids. Make sure you use 100% pure maple syrup. In addition to the Power Punch nutrients listed below, each serving is a good source of the following (based on percent of Daily Values): 11% of protein, 17% of riboflavin/B2, 10% of folate, 11% of iron, 11% of magnesium, and 17% of zinc.

Crust:
Butter-flavored cooking spray
20 saltine crackers
1½ tablespoons fat-free margarine

Filling:
⅓ cup brown sugar
2 tablespoons all-purpose flour
1 teaspoon vanilla extract
1 tablespoon fat-free margarine
½ cup egg substitute
1 cup maple syrup
1 ⅓ cups walnuts

Preheat oven to 350°. Spray a pie pan with cooking spray and wipe with a paper towel to spread evenly and absorb the excess.

Use a food processor to make crumbs from crackers. Combine the crumbs and margarine, and mix until crumbs are evenly moistened. Press them into the bottom and part-way up the sides of the pan.

Combine the brown sugar and flour. Then add the vanilla, margarine and egg substitute. Then add the syrup. Finally, stir in the walnuts. Pour into pie crust and bake for 45 minutes at 350°.

Nutritional information per serving (based on 8 servings):

The Basics	Power Punch	% Daily Value
Calories 322	Copper (0.4 mg)	20%
Protein 5 g	Manganese (2.1 mg)	105%
Carbohydrate 46 g	Omega-3 fatty acids (1.8 g)	
Total fat 14 g	Omega-6 fatty acids (7.8 g)	
% Calories from fat 38		
Saturated fat 1 g		
Dietary Fiber 2 g		
Cholesterol 0 mg		
Sodium 171 mg		

Black Forest Pie
Makes 1 Pie (8 Slices)

If you love chocolate-covered cherries, this is the pie for you! In addition to the Power Punch nutrients listed below, each serving is a good source of the following (based on percent of Daily Values): 12% of fiber, 12% of vitamin A, 11% of iron, and 15% of potassium.

Crust:
Butter-flavored cooking spray
12 reduced-fat Oreo cookies
⅔ cup instant skim milk powder
¼ cup powdered sugar
2-3 tablespoons fat-free margarine

Filling:
6 tablespoons unsweetened cocoa powder
¼ cup all-purpose flour
¼ cup fat-free egg substitute
½ teaspoon almond extract
1 tablespoon brandy
1 (14 ounce) can fat-free sweetened condensed milk
1 (16 ounce) bag of frozen, unsweetened, pitted cherries, thawed

Topping:
½ cup nonfat sour cream
¼ teaspoon almond extract
¼ cup powdered sugar

Preheat oven to 325°. Spray a pie pan with cooking spray and wipe with a paper towel to spread evenly and absorb the excess.

Use a food processor to make crumbs from the cookies. Combine the cookie crumbs, milk powder, and powdered sugar in a bowl. Then add 2 tablespoons of margarine and mix until crumbs are evenly moistened. If the crumbs are still too dry to press into the pan, add a little more margarine. But don't add too much margarine – you don't want the crumbs to stick together and become pasty. When the crumbs are ready, press them into the bottom and part-way up the sides of the pan.

Combine the cocoa and flour. Then add the egg substitute, almond extract, brandy and milk, and mix well. Gently stir in cherries. Pour into pie crust and bake for 1 hour.

Allow the pie to cool for about an hour. Combine the topping ingredients and spread evenly over the pie.

Nutritional information per serving (based on 8 servings):

The Basics	Power Punch	% Daily Value
Calories 355	Protein (11.24 g)	22%
Protein 11 g	Riboflavin/B2 (0.5 mg)	29%
Carbohydrate 71 g	Calcium (248 mg)	25%
Total fat 3 g	Phosphorus (206 mg)	21%
% Calories from fat 7	Cherries (56 g)	
Saturated fat 1 g		
Dietary Fiber 3 g		
Cholesterol 4 mg		
Sodium 140 mg		

Orange Dream Pie
Makes 1 Pie (8 Slices)

This frozen delight combines orange and vanilla to make a creamy, dreamy classic. In addition to the Power Punch nutrients listed below, each serving is a good source of the following (based on percent of Daily Values): 13% of protein, 10% of vitamin A, 19% of riboflavin/B2, 15% of vitamin D, and 11% of potassium.

Crust:
Butter-flavored cooking spray
12 reduced-fat vanilla sandwich cookies
⅔ cup instant skim milk powder
¼ cup powdered sugar
2 tablespoons fat-free margarine

Filling:
½ cup frozen orange juice concentrate, thawed
1 cup canned, evaporated fat-free milk
⅓ cup instant skim milk powder
1 (3.4 ounce) box instant vanilla pudding mix

Spray a pie pan with cooking spray and wipe with a paper towel to spread evenly and absorb the excess.

Use a food processor to make crumbs from the cookies. Combine the crumbs, milk powder, and sugar. Then add the margarine and mix until crumbs are evenly moistened. Press them into the bottom and part-way up the sides of the pan.

Combine the filling ingredients and mix well. Pour into pie crust and refrigerate until somewhat set. Then put in the freezer. Once frozen, cover with foil to keep fresh.

Nutritional information per serving (based on 8 servings):

The Basics	Power Punch	% Daily Value
Calories 226	Vitamin C (25 mg)	42%
Protein 6 g	Calcium (205 mg)	20%
Carbohydrate 46 g	Phosphorus (266 mg)	27%
Total fat 2 g		
% Calories from fat 8		
Saturated fat 0 g		
Dietary Fiber 1 g		
Cholesterol 2 mg		
Sodium 360 mg		

Pumpkin Pie
Makes 1 Pie (8 Slices)

Traditional pumpkin pies are high in vitamin A. This one is also high in calcium. In addition to the Power Punch nutrients listed below, each serving is a good source of the following (based on percent of Daily Values): 19% of protein, 12% of fiber, 12% of manganese, and 18% of phosphorus.

Crust:
Butter-flavored cooking spray
1 ¼ cups graham cracker crumbs
¼ cup sugar
2 tablespoons fat-free margarine

Filling:
1 (15 ounce) can solid-pack pumpkin
1 (14 ounce) can fat-free sweetened condensed milk
½ cup fat-free egg substitute
½ cup instant skim milk powder
1 teaspoon cinnamon
½ teaspoon ginger
½ teaspoon nutmeg
1 teaspoon vanilla extract

Preheat oven to 325°. Spray a pie pan with cooking spray, wiping with a paper towel to spread evenly and absorb the excess.

Combine the crumbs, sugar and margarine, and mix until crumbs are evenly moistened. Press them into the bottom and part-way up the sides of the pan.

Combine the filling ingredients and mix well. Pour into pie crust and bake for 1 hour and 5 minutes. Cool completely.

Power Desserts

Nutritional information per serving (based on 8 servings):

The Basics	Power Punch	% Daily Value
Calories 287	Vitamin A (7976 IU)	160%
Protein 10 g	Riboflavin/B2 (0.56 mg)	33%
Carbohydrate 57 g	Calcium (222 mg)	22%
Total fat 2 g	Pumpkin (53 g)	
% Calories from fat 7		
Saturated fat 0 g		
Dietary Fiber 3 g		
Cholesterol 4 mg		
Sodium 245 mg		

Blueberry Crumb Pie
Makes 1 Pie (8 Slices)

This pie is packed with 2 pounds of anti-oxidant-rich blueberries. And because it uses frozen blueberries you can enjoy this delicious, nutritious pie year-round. In addition to the Power Punch nutrients listed below, each serving is a good source of the following (based on percent of Daily Values): 12% of protein, 17% of thiamin/B1, 13% of riboflavin/B2, 10% of niacin/B3, 11% of folate, 14% of copper, 16% of magnesium, and 15% of phosphorus.

Crust/Crumb Base:
⅔ cup brown sugar   3 tablespoons wheat germ
⅔ cup quick oats   ⅓ cup all-purpose flour
2 tablespoons fat-free margarine
¼ teaspoon salt

Crust:
Butter-flavored cooking spray
1 cup of base crumbs   ¼ cup all-purpose flour

Filling:
¾ cup sugar
1 tablespoon cornstarch
¼ cup all-purpose flour
¼ teaspoon cinnamon
2 tablespoons lemon juice
2 (16-ounce each) bags of frozen blueberries, thawed

Crumb Topping:
Remaining base crumbs
1 cup sliced almonds
Preheat oven to 350°. Combine all crust/crumb base ingredients, except margarine, and mix well. Add margarine and mix until crumbs are evenly moistened. Remove 1 cup of crumbs for crust.

Spray a deep-dish pie pan with cooking spray and wipe with a paper towel to spread evenly and absorb the excess. For the crust, combine 1 cup of crumbs with flour and mix until crumbs are evenly moistened. Press these crumbs into the bottom and part-way up the sides of the pan.

For the filling, combine sugar, cornstarch, flour, and cinnamon in a large bowl and mix well. Add the lemon juice and mix well. Gently stir in blueberries until evenly mixed. Pour into pie crust and bake for 15 minutes.

While pie is baking, crush the sliced almonds into smaller bits. Stir the almonds into the remaining crust/crumb base crumbs. After the pie has baked for 15 minutes, remove it from the oven. Sprinkle with crumb topping, and return to oven. Bake for 1 hour. Note: you may want to put foil under the pie while it bakes in case it bubbles over the edge of the pie pan.

Nutritional information per serving (based on 8 servings):

The Basics	Power Punch	% Daily Value
Calories 360	Dietary fiber (5.58 g)	22%
Protein 6 g	Vitamin E (6.12 IU)	20%
Carbohydrate 69 g	Manganese (1.07 mg)	53%
Total fat 8 g	Blueberries (113 g)	
% Calories from fat 19		
Saturated fat 1 g		
Dietary Fiber 6 g		
Cholesterol 0 mg		
Sodium 105 mg		

Chocolate Malt Pie
Makes 1 Pie (8 Slices)

This fabulous, cookie-crusted pie is creamy and classic. The chocolate-malt combo will take you back to the soda fountain days – minus most of the fat! In addition to the Power Punch nutrients listed below, each serving is a good source of the following (based on percent of Daily Values): 15% of protein, 13% of vitamin D, and 11% of potassium.

Crust:
Butter-flavored cooking spray
12 reduced-fat Oreo cookies
¼ cup instant skim milk powder
¼ cup powdered sugar
2 tablespoons fat-free margarine

Filling:
1 (12 ounce) can evaporated fat-free milk
¼ cup instant skim milk powder
½ cup malted milk powder
1 (3.4 ounce) box instant vanilla pudding mix
1 tablespoon unsweetened cocoa powder

Spray a pie pan with cooking spray and wipe with a paper towel to spread evenly and absorb the excess.

Use a food processor to make crumbs from the cookies. Combine the crumbs, milk powder, and sugar. Then add the margarine and mix until crumbs are evenly moistened. Press them into the bottom and part-way up the sides of the pan.

Combine the filling ingredients and mix well. Pour into pie crust and refrigerate until somewhat set. Then put in the freezer. Once frozen, cover with foil to keep fresh.

Nutritional information per serving (based on 8 servings):

The Basics	Power Punch	% Daily Value
Calories 236	Riboflavin/B2 (0.4 mg)	24%
Protein 8 g	Calcium (223 mg)	22%
Carbohydrate 44 g	Phosphorus (231 mg)	23%
Total fat 4 g		
% Calories from fat 13		
Saturated fat 1 g		
Dietary Fiber 1 g		
Cholesterol 5 mg		
Sodium 271 mg		

Caramel Applesauce Pie
Makes 1 Pie (8 Slices)

This very sweet pie combines the wonderful flavors of caramel and apples. In addition to the Power Punch nutrients listed below, each serving is a good source of potassium (12% of daily value).

Crust:
Butter-flavored cooking spray
1 cup graham cracker crumbs
¼ cup sugar
⅓ cup instant skim milk powder
2 tablespoons fat-free margarine

Filling:
½ cup fat-free caramel sauce (divided)
2 cups unsweetened applesauce
1 (14 ounce) can fat-free sweetened condensed milk
½ teaspoon cinnamon
½ cup instant skim milk powder
¼ cup fat-free egg substitute
1 tablespoon cornstarch
1 teaspoon vanilla extract
½ teaspoon lemon extract

Preheat oven to 325°. Spray a pie pan with cooking spray and wipe with a paper towel to spread evenly and absorb the excess.

Combine the crumbs, sugar, and milk powder. Add the margarine and mix until crumbs are evenly moistened. Reserve ½ cup of crumbs for topping. Press remaining crumbs into the bottom and part-way up the sides of the pan.

Drizzle ¼ cup of caramel sauce over the pie crust.
Combine the remaining filling ingredients (all except the
remaining caramel sauce) and mix well. Pour into pie crust
over caramel and sprinkle ½ cup of crumbs on top. Bake
for 1 hour and 15 minutes. Cool completely. Then drizzle
remaining ¼ cup of caramel sauce over the top of the pie.

Nutritional information per serving (based on 8 servings):

The Basics	Power Punch	% Daily Value
Calories 349	Protein (9.76 g)	20%
Protein 10 g	Riboflavin/B2 (0.5 mg)	30%
Carbohydrate 73 g	Calcium (265 mg)	27%
Total fat 2 g	Phosphorus (204 mg)	20%
% Calories from fat 4		
Saturated fat 0 g		
Dietary Fiber 1 g		
Cholesterol 5 mg		
Sodium 266 mg		

Power Desserts

Breads, Muffins & Breakfast Sweets

Banana Pistachio Coffee Cake
Makes 1 Coffee Cake (12 Slices)

This combination of banana and pistachios along with the pudding topping makes for a very unique and tasty coffee cake. In addition to the Power Punch nutrients listed below, each serving is a good source of the following (based on percent of Daily Values): 17% of protein, 13% of fiber, 11% of niacin (B3), 16% of folate, 14% of calcium, 17% of copper, 15% of iron, 11% of magnesium, 17% of phosphorus, 17% of potassium, 17% of selenium.

Batter:
Butter-flavored cooking spray
2 ¾ cups all-purpose flour
½ teaspoon baking soda
½ teaspoon salt
1 teaspoon vanilla extract
3 cups mashed banana (about 6 medium bananas)
1 ¾ cups brown sugar
¼ cup egg substitute

Pudding Topping:
1 (3.4 ounce) box instant pistachio pudding mix
1 (12 ounce) can evaporated fat-free milk
1 teaspoon vanilla extract
1 cup pistachio kernels

Preheat oven to 325°. Spray a 13x9-inch pan with cooking spray and wipe with a paper towel to spread evenly and absorb the excess.

Combine the flour, baking soda, and salt in a medium bowl. In a large bowl, combine the vanilla, banana, sugar,

and egg substitute. Add the dry to the wet and mix well.
Spread the batter in the pan evenly.

Combine all topping ingredients, except nuts. Spoon in
thick stripes over the batter and swirl with a spoon or knife.
Sprinkle nuts over batter/topping. Bake for 1 hour.

Nutritional information per serving (based on 12 servings):

The Basics	Power Punch	% Daily Value
Calories 399	Thiamin/B1 (0.3 mg)	23%
Protein 8 g	Riboflavin/B2 (0.4mg)	23%
Carbohydrate 81 g	Vitamin B6 (0.5 mg)	27%
Total fat 6 g	Manganese (0.5 mg)	26%
% Calories from fat 12		
Saturated fat 1 g		
Dietary Fiber 3 g		
Cholesterol 0 mg		
Sodium 339 mg		

Sweet Potato Muffins
Makes 12 muffins

These tasty muffins make a great snack. In addition to the Power Punch nutrients listed below, each serving is a good source of the following (based on percent of Daily Values): 12% of fiber, 10% of riboflavin (B2), and 12% of manganese.

Batter:
Butter-flavored cooking spray
1 cup whole wheat flour
½ cup all-purpose flour
½ teaspoon baking powder
½ teaspoon baking soda
½ teaspoon cinnamon
½ teaspoon nutmeg
½ teaspoon salt
¾ cup brown sugar
¼ cup fat-free egg substitute
1 teaspoon vanilla extract
½ cup plain, nonfat yogurt
4 cups peeled, uncooked, shredded sweet potatoes
   (about 2 medium potatoes)

Topping:
2 tablespoons brown sugar
¼ teaspoon cinnamon

Preheat oven to 350°. Spray a 12-muffin tin with cooking spray and wipe with a paper towel to spread evenly and absorb the excess.

Combine the flours, baking powder, baking soda, spices, and salt in a medium bowl. In a large bowl, combine the sugar, egg substitute, vanilla, and yogurt. Add the dry to

86

the wet and mix well. Stir in the shredded sweet potato.
Spoon batter into muffin tin.

Combine topping ingredients and sprinkle over the muffins.
Bake for 25 minutes. Cool in pan for 5 minutes before
removing the muffins from the tin.

Nutritional information per serving (based on 12 servings):

The Basics	Power Punch	% Daily Value
Calories 175	Vitamin A (8920 IU)	178%
Protein 4 g	Sweet potatoes (44 g)	
Carbohydrate 39 g		
Total fat 1 g		
% Calories from fat 3		
Saturated fat 0 g		
Dietary Fiber 3 g		
Cholesterol 0 mg		
Sodium 198 mg		

Raspberry Peach Breakfast Bars
Makes 9 Bars

These delicious bars were inspired by our friend Toni who had a craving during her pregnancy for something that combined raspberry and peach flavors. In addition to the Power Punch nutrients listed below, each serving is a good source of the following (based on percent of Daily Values): 12% of vitamin A, 16% of vitamin D, 10% of vitamin E, 15% of folate, 11% of iron, 16% of magnesium, 16% of potassium, and 15% of zinc.

Crust:
Butter-flavored cooking spray
½ cup all-purpose flour
1 ½ cups quick oats
⅔ cup brown sugar
⅔ cup wheat germ
1 cup instant skim milk powder
¼ cup fat-free margarine

Filling:
1 (12 ounce) can evaporated fat-free milk
1 (3.4 ounce) package instant lemon pudding mix
1 (10 ounce) jar peach preserves
1 (12 ounce) bag frozen, unsweetened raspberries, thawed

Preheat oven to 350°. Spray an 8 ½-inch square pan with cooking spray and wipe with a paper towel to spread evenly and absorb the excess.

Combine the flour, oats, sugar, wheat germ and milk powder. Then add the margarine and mix until crumbs are evenly moist. Reserve 1 cup of crumbs. Press remaining crumbs into bottom of pan.

Combine evaporated milk, preserves and pudding mix and mix well. Gently stir in raspberries. Pour and spread evenly over crust. Sprinkle with reserved cup of crumbs. Bake for 50 minutes. Cool completely.

Nutritional information per serving (based on 9 servings):

The Basics	Power Punch	% Daily Value
Calories 370	Protein (11 g)	22%
Protein 11 g	Dietary fiber (4.9 g)	20%
Carbohydrate 79 g	Thiamin/B1 (0.3 mg)	21%
Total fat 2 g	Riboflavin/B2 (0.4 mg)	25%
% Calories from fat 5	Calcium (234 mg)	23%
Saturated fat 0 g	Manganese (2.5 mg)	126%
Dietary Fiber 5 g	Phosphorus (401 mg)	40%
Cholesterol 1 mg	Raspberries (38 g)	
Sodium 300 mg		

Blueberry Coffee Cake
Makes 1 Coffee Cake (8 Wedges)

This is a sweet way to start the day! In addition to the Power Punch nutrients listed below, each serving is a good source of the following (based on percent of Daily Values): 13% of Vitamin A, 15% of thiamin (B1), 10% of manganese, 11% of potassium, and 11% of selenium.

Batter:
1 cup all-purpose flour
2 tablespoons cornstarch
⅔ cup instant skim milk powder
½ teaspoon baking powder
¼ teaspoon salt
½ teaspoon nutmeg
⅔ cup sugar
¼ cup fat-free margarine
1 tablespoon lemon zest
¼ cup fat-free egg substitute
½ cup nonfat sour cream
¼ cup lemon juice
1 (14 ounce) can sweetened condensed milk
1 (16 ounce) bag frozen, unsweetened blueberries, thawed

Icing:
⅓ cup powdered sugar
1 tablespoon lemon juice

Preheat oven to 325°. Cover the bottom of a 10-inch springform pan with wax paper and then lock the sides of the pan in place.

Combine the flour, cornstarch, milk powder, baking powder, nutmeg, and salt in a medium bowl. In a large bowl, combine all remaining batter ingredients, except the blueberries. Add the dry to the wet and mix well. Gently fold in the blueberries. Pour into the pan and bake for 1 hour and 25 minutes. Allow the cake to cool completely. Then remove the sides of the pan.

Combine icing ingredients and drizzle over cake.

Nutritional information per serving (based on 8 servings):

The Basics	Power Punch	% Daily Value
Calories 360	Protein (9.8 g)	20%
Protein 10 g	Riboflavin/B2 (0.5 mg)	32%
Carbohydrate 79 g	Calcium (261 mg)	26%
Total fat 1 g	Phosphorus (221 mg)	22%
% Calories from fat 2	Blueberries (57 g)	
Saturated fat 0 g		
Dietary Fiber 2 g		
Cholesterol 6 mg		
Sodium 262 mg		

Strawberry Walnut Bread
Makes 1 Loaf (10 Slices)

The contrasting flavors and textures of the berries and nuts make this bread a great, easy snack. In addition to the Power Punch nutrients listed below, each serving is a good source of the following (based on percent of Daily Values): 12% of protein, 11% of fiber, 14% of thiamin (B1), 12% of riboflavin (B2), 13% of folate, 16% of copper, 12% of phosphorus, 11% of selenium.

Batter:
Butter-flavored cooking spray
Flour for dusting pan
1 ½ cup all-purpose flour
½ teaspoon baking soda
½ teaspoon salt
1 teaspoon cinnamon
1 cup sugar
¾ cup evaporated fat-free milk
1 ⅓ cups chopped walnuts
1 (16 ounce) bag frozen, unsweetened strawberries, thawed

Preheat oven to 325°. Spray a loaf pan with cooking spray and wipe with a paper towel to spread evenly and absorb the excess. Dust pan with flour until coated on bottom and sides. Discard excess flour.

Combine the flour, baking soda, salt, and cinnamon in a medium bowl. In a large bowl, combine the sugar and milk. Add the dry to the wet and mix well. Stir in the strawberries and walnuts. Pour into the pan and bake for 1 hour and 25 minutes. Allow the bread to cool. Then remove from pan.

Nutritional information per serving (based on 10 servings):

The Basics	Power Punch	% Daily Value
Calories 282	Manganese (0.8 mg)	40%
Protein 6 g	Omega 3 fatty acids (1.5 g)	
Carbohydrate 43 g	Omega 6 fatty acids (6.2 g)	
Total fat 11 g	Strawberries (46 g)	
% Calories from fat 33		
Saturated fat 1 g		
Dietary Fiber 3 g		
Cholesterol 0 mg		
Sodium 205 mg		

Orange Cranberry Muffins
Makes 12 Muffins

These extra tangy muffins work as dessert or as a snack. In addition to the Power Punch nutrients listed below, each serving is a good source of the following (based on percent of Daily Values): 11% of fiber, 11% of thiamin (B1), 10% of riboflavin (B2), 10% of folate, 16% of selenium.

Batter:
1 cup all-purpose flour
1 cup whole wheat flour
½ teaspoon salt
½ teaspoon baking powder
½ teaspoon baking soda
¼ cup fat-free egg substitute
1 ½ cups sugar
1 tablespoon vanilla extract
¼ cup water
¼ cup frozen orange juice concentrate, thawed
2 tablespoons fat-free margarine
Zest from one orange
1 (12 ounce) bag fresh cranberries

Icing:
½ cup powdered sugar
¼ cup frozen orange juice concentrate, thawed

Preheat oven to 325°. Rinse the cranberries in a colander, drain, and pat until mostly dry. Coarsely chop the cranberries in a food processor.

Combine the flours, salt, baking powder and soda in a medium bowl. In a large bowl, combine the remaining batter ingredients, except the cranberries. Add the dry to wet, and mix well. Stir in the cranberries.

Insert cupcake liners in a 12-muffin tin. Spoon the batter into the liners. Bake for 50 minutes. Cool completely.

Combine the icing ingredients. Poke several holes in each muffin and drizzle icing over them.

Nutritional information per serving (based on 12 servings):

The Basics	Power Punch	% Daily Value
Calories 227	Vitamin C (20 mg)	34%
Protein 3 g	Manganese (0.5 mg)	25%
Carbohydrate 53 g	Cranberries (28 g)	
Total fat 0 g		
% Calories from fat 1		
Saturated fat 0 g		
Dietary Fiber 3 g		
Cholesterol 0 mg		
Sodium 197 mg		

Cinnamon Pumpkin Raisin Coffee Cake
Makes 1 Coffee Cake (15 Servings)

If you like cinnamon and raisins, you'll love this coffee cake, which is topped with a rich cinnamon swirl. In addition to the Power Punch nutrients listed below, each serving is a good source of the following (based on percent of Daily Values): 10% of protein, 15% of fiber, 15% of thiamin (B1), 15% of riboflavin (B2), 10% of copper, 13% of iron, and 10% of potassium.

Batter:
Butter-flavored cooking spray
1 cup canned carrot juice
3 cups raisins
1 cup quick oats
2 cups all-purpose flour
1 teaspoon baking powder
1 teaspoon baking soda
½ teaspoon salt
½ cup fat-free egg substitute
2 cups sugar
1 (15 ounce) can solid pack pumpkin
2 teaspoons vanilla extract

Cinnamon Swirl:
1 cup brown sugar
2 tablespoons all-purpose flour
2 teaspoons cinnamon
⅛ teaspoon salt
2 tablespoons fat-free margarine
1 tablespoon plain, nonfat yogurt

96

Soak the raisins in the carrot juice in the refrigerator, uncovered, for two to three hours, stirring once or twice.

Preheat oven to 325°. Spray a 13x9-inch pan with cooking spray and wipe with a paper towel to spread evenly and absorb the excess.

Combine the oats, flour, baking powder, baking soda, and salt in a medium bowl. In a large bowl, combine the sugar, egg substitute, pumpkin, and vanilla. Add the dry to the wet and mix well. Stir in the raisins and carrot juice. Spread batter in pan evenly.

For the swirl, combine the brown sugar, flour, cinnamon and salt, and mix well. Add the margarine and yogurt, and mix well. Spoon in five thick stripes across the width (i.e., short side) over the batter and swirl with a knife. Bake for 1 hour.

Nutritional information per serving (based on 15 servings):

The Basics	Power Punch	% Daily Value
Calories 355	Vitamin A (6175 IU)	124%
Protein 5 g	Manganese (0.5 mg)	26%
Carbohydrate 85 g	Pumpkin (28 g)	
Total fat 1 g	Raisins (29 g)	
% Calories from fat 2		
Saturated fat 0 g		
Dietary Fiber 4 g		
Cholesterol 0 mg		
Sodium 258 mg		

Caramel Corn Muffins
Makes 12 Muffins

These delicious corny muffins can be served with dinner or after it. In addition to the Power Punch nutrients listed below, each serving is a good source of the following (based on percent of Daily Values): 10% of thiamin (B1), 11% of riboflavin (B2), 12% of folate, and 11% of manganese.

Batter:
1½ cup all-purpose flour
2 teaspoons baking powder
¼ teaspoon salt
¾ cup dark brown sugar
2 teaspoons vanilla extract
¼ cup fat-free egg substitute
¼ cup fat-free margarine
2 (15.25-ounce each) cans yellow corn, no salt added, drained

Preheat oven to 325°. Put muffin liners in a 12-muffin tin. Combine the flour, baking powder, and salt in a medium bowl. In a large bowl, combine remaining ingredients, except corn, and mix well. Add the dry to the wet and mix well. Stir in the drained corn. Spoon batter into muffin liners. Bake for 50 minutes.

Nutritional information per serving (based on 12 servings):

The Basics	Power Punch	% Daily Value
Calories 149	Yellow corn (41 g)	
Protein 3 g		
Carbohydrate 33 g		
Total fat 1 g		
% Calories from fat 3		
Saturated fat 0 g		
Dietary Fiber 1 g		
Cholesterol 0 mg		
Sodium 178 mg		

98

Blueberry Lemon Muffins
Makes 12 Muffins

These tasty muffins are so easy because they start with a mix. In addition to the Power Punch nutrients listed below, each serving is a good source of the following (based on percent of Daily Values): 10% of protein, 13% of riboflavin (B2), and 11% of calcium.

Batter:
1 (15.6 ounce) box of lemon poppy seed bread/muffin mix
1 cup evaporated fat-free milk, canned
½ cup fat-free egg substitute
1 (16 ounce) bag frozen, unsweetened blueberries, thawed

Preheat oven to 350°. Put muffin liners in a 12-muffin tin. Combine all batter ingredients, except blueberries, and mix well. Gently fold in blueberries. Spoon batter into liners. Bake for 50 minutes.

Nutritional information per serving (based on 12 servings):

The Basics	Power Punch	% Daily Value
Calories 200	Blueberries (38 g)	
Protein 5 g		
Carbohydrate 34 g		
Total fat 5 g		
% Calories from fat 22		
Saturated fat 1 g		
Dietary Fiber 2 g		
Cholesterol 1 mg		
Sodium		

Other Desserts

Pumpkin Cheesecake
Makes 1 Cheesecake (12 slices)

This spiced cheesecake is incredibly smooth and creamy. You'd never know that it's so low in fat.

Crust:
Butter-flavored cooking spray
1 ½ cups graham cracker crumbs
¼ cup powdered sugar
¼ cup plain nonfat yogurt

Filling:
3 (8-ounce each) tubs of soft fat-free cream cheese
1 ½ cups sugar
1 (15 ounce) can solid pack pumpkin
3 tablespoons cornstarch
2 ½ teaspoons ginger
1 tablespoon cinnamon
½ teaspoon nutmeg
1 tablespoon vanilla extract
½ cup fat-free egg substitute

Topping:
1 cup nonfat sour cream
¼ cup sugar
½ teaspoon cinnamon

Preheat oven to 300°. Spray a 9-inch springform pan with cooking spray and wipe with a paper towel to spread evenly and absorb the excess.

Combine the remaining crust ingredients. Press into the bottom (only) of the pan (not up the side).

Combine cream cheese and sugar in a large bowl and mix well. Add pumpkin, cornstarch and spices, and mix well. Add vanilla and egg substitute, and mix well. Pour filling over crust. Bake for 1 hour. Cool cheesecake completely in pan.

When completely cool, remove sides of the pan. Combine topping ingredients and mix well. Spread topping over cheesecake.

Nutritional information per serving (based 12 servings):

The Basics	Power Punch	% Daily Value
Calories 290	Protein (12.5 g)	25%
Protein 12 g	Vitamin A (6140 IU)	123%
Carbohydrate 56 g	Riboflavin/B2 (0.8 mg)	49%
Total fat 2 g	Calcium (234 mg)	23%
% Calories from fat 6	Phosphorus (299 mg)	30%
Saturated fat 0 g	Pumpkin (35 g)	
Dietary Fiber 2 g		
Cholesterol 6 mg		
Sodium 407 mg		

Cranberry Cheesecake
Makes 1 Cheesecake (12 slices)

This cheesecake is so pretty with its pink filling and red-dotted topping. And it tastes as good as it looks!

Crust:
Butter-flavored cooking spray
1 ½ cups graham cracker crumbs
¼ cup powdered sugar
¼ cup plain nonfat yogurt

Filling:
1 (11.5 ounce) can cranberry juice cocktail concentrate
1 (3.4 ounce) package instant lemon pudding mix
3 (8-ounce each) tubs of soft fat-free cream cheese
3 tablespoons cornstarch
½ cup powdered sugar
½ cup fat-free egg substitute

Topping:
1 cup nonfat sour cream
¼ cup sugar
1 (6 ounce) package dried, sweetened cranberries

Preheat oven to 300°. Spray a 9-inch springform pan with cooking spray and wipe with a paper towel to spread evenly and absorb the excess.

Combine the remaining crust ingredients. Press into the bottom of the pan (but not up the side).

Combine the juice concentrate and the pudding mix in a small bowl and mix well. Combine cream cheese and cornstarch in a large bowl and mix well. Add egg substitute to cream cheese mixture, and mix well. Add

powdered sugar to cream cheese mixture and mix well.
Add the juice/pudding mixture to the cream cheese
mixture and mix well.

Pour filling over crust. Bake for 1 hour. Cool cheesecake
completely in pan.

When completely cool, remove sides of the pan. Combine
sour cream and sugar, mixing well. Stir in cranberries and
spread topping over cheesecake.

Nutritional information per serving (based on 12 servings):

The Basics	Power Punch	% Daily Value
Calories 339	Protein (11.9 g)	24%
Protein 12 g	Vitamin A (1066 IU)	21%
Carbohydrate 69 g	Riboflavin/B2 (0.8 mg)	50%
Total fat 2 g	Calcium (222 mg)	22%
% Calories from fat 5	Phosphorus (302 mg)	30%
Saturated fat 0 g	Cranberries/juice (49 g)	
Dietary Fiber 2 g		
Cholesterol 6 mg		
Sodium 503 mg		

Milk Chocolate Peanut Fudge
Makes 12 Servings

I've always enjoyed a good challenge. And making fudge with no butter and with any redeeming nutritional value was certainly just that. I think this recipe was worth all of my experimenting! In addition to the Power Punch nutrients listed below, each serving is a good source of the following (based on percent of Daily Values): 14% of fiber, 16% of riboflavin (B2), 10% of vitamin E, 10% of folate, 19% of copper, 17% of magnesium, 13% of molybdenum, 14% of potassium, and 16% of zinc.

Ingredients:
Butter-flavored cooking spray
1 (14 ounce) can fat-free sweetened condensed milk
1 cup instant skim milk powder
1 tablespoon fat-free margarine
1 tablespoon fat-free evaporated skim milk
1 teaspoon vanilla extract
1 (16 ounce) box powdered sugar
½ cup unsweetened cocoa powder
1 (12 ounce) can lightly salted cocktail peanuts

Spray an 8-or 9-inch square pan with cooking spray and wipe with a paper towel to spread evenly and absorb the excess.

Combine the condensed milk, milk powder and margarine in a large non-metal bowl, and mix well. Microwave uncovered for 30 seconds. Add evaporated milk and vanilla, and mix well until smooth and powdered milk is dissolved. Add the powdered sugar and cocoa powder, mixing well. Mixture will be stiff. Then add the peanuts and mix well. Spread fudge into pan and let sit in refrigerator, uncovered, for 24 hours.

106

Nutritional information per serving (based on 12 servings):

The Basics	Power Punch	% Daily Value
Calories 439	Protein (13.2 g)	26%
Protein 13 g	Niacin/B3 (4.3 mg)	21%
Carbohydrate 68 g	Calcium (197 mg)	20%
Total fat 14 g	Manganese (0.6 mg)	29%
% Calories from fat 28	Phosphorus (279 mg)	28%
Saturated fat 2 g		
Dietary Fiber 3 g		
Cholesterol 3 mg		
Sodium 199 mg		

Maple Nut Fudge
Makes 12 Servings

This sweet treat is the perfect confection for those of you with a very sweet tooth and a desire to increase your intake of the omega fatty acids. In addition to the Power Punch nutrients listed below, each serving is a good source of the following (based on percent of Daily Values): 18% of protein, 10% of thiamin (B1), 17% of riboflavin (B2), 14% of magnesium, 11% of molybdenum, and 10% of potassium.

Ingredients:
Butter-flavored cooking spray
1 (14 ounce) can fat-free sweetened condensed milk
1 cup plus 2 tablespoons instant skim milk powder
1 tablespoon fat-free margarine
½ teaspoon vanilla extract
¼ teaspoon maple extract
1 (16 ounce) box plus ½ cup powdered sugar
2 ½ cups chopped walnuts

Spray an 8- or 9-inch square pan with cooking spray and wipe with a paper towel to spread evenly and absorb the excess.

Combine the condensed milk, milk powder, and margarine in a large non-metal bowl, and mix well. Microwave uncovered for 30 seconds. Add the extracts and mix until smooth and powdered milk is dissolved. Add the powdered sugar and mix well. Mixture will be stiff. Then add the walnuts and mix well. Spread fudge into pan and let sit in refrigerator, uncovered, for 24 hours.

Nutritional information per serving (based on 12 servings):

The Basics	Power Punch	% Daily Value
Calories 446	Calcium (198 mg)	20%
Protein 9 g	Copper (0.4 mg)	21%
Carbohydrate 69 g	Manganese (0.9 mg)	43%
Total fat 16 g	Phosphorus (227 mg)	23%
% Calories from fat 32	Omega-3 fatty acids (2.3 g)	
Saturated fat 2 g	Omega-6 fatty acids (9.5 g)	
Dietary Fiber 2 g		
Cholesterol 3 mg		
Sodium 78 mg		

Tiramisu
Makes 8 Servings

This classic dessert was a big hit with our dear neighbors, Ed and Ethel. But don't eat and drive – there is a good dose of alcohol in this treat! And if you want to make this fat-free and cholesterol-free, use slices of angel food cake instead of the lady fingers. In addition to the Power Punch nutrients listed below, each serving is a good source of the following (based on percent of Daily Values): 17% of vitamin A, and 16% of vitamin D.

Filling:
1 (12 ounce) can evaporated fat-free milk
1 (8 ounce) package fat-free cream cheese
½ cup instant skim milk powder
1 (3.4 ounce) package instant French vanilla pudding mix
½ cup powdered sugar
1 (8 ounce) container fat-free frozen whipped topping,
   thawed

Other Ingredients:
2 (3-ounce each) packages ladyfingers
½ cup Kahlua liqueur (or ¼ cup Kahlua plus ¼ cup crème
   de cacao)
1 tablespoon unsweetened cocoa powder

Combine first three filling ingredients in a large bowl and mix well. Add the pudding mix and mix well. Add the powdered sugar and mix well. Gently fold in the whipped topping.

In a 12 cup serving dish or container, line the bottom with one package of ladyfingers. Drizzle ¼ cup of liqueur over the ladyfingers. Spread half of filling over the ladyfingers. Layer the other package of ladyfingers evenly over the topping. Drizzle with remaining ¼ cup of liqueur. Spread remaining filling over top. Sprinkle cocoa over the top.

Nutritional information per serving (based on 8 servings):

The Basics	Power Punch	% Daily Value
Calories 337	Protein (11 g)	22%
Protein 11 g	Riboflavin/B2 (0.4 mg)	23%
Carbohydrate 60 g	Calcium (266 mg)	27%
Total fat 2 g	Phosphorus (356 mg)	36%
% Calories from fat 6		
Saturated fat 1 g		
Dietary Fiber 0 g		
Cholesterol 81 mg		
Sodium 442 mg		

Tropical Banana Crumb Cobbler a la Mode
Makes 12 Servings

This unique dessert was completely inspired by a dessert special made by Pastry Chef April-Sue Kahuhu at the Hotel Hana Maui, the world's best hotel as rated by my husband and me. Chef Kahuhu's banana cobbler a la mode was one of the best desserts I've ever tasted, so I decided to attempt a Power Dessert version. Hawaiian bananas are different from mainland bananas – they're more firm and just a little tangy. So, assuming most readers will have access only to mainland bananas, my recipe calls for using under-ripe bananas for texture, and strawberries and a little pineapple to add the tang. I also used real vanilla bean to add to the richness – it takes a little extra time, but it is worth it. My husband and I both love this Power Dessert version, although it is no match for Chef Kahuhu's creation. For that, you'll have to pack your bags and head for Hawaii! The nutritional information provided below uses store-bought vanilla ice cream. But you can increase the calcium content by using the vanilla ice cream recipe on page 126. In addition to the Power Punch nutrients listed below, each serving is a good source of the following (based on percent of Daily Values): 17% of protein, 19% of fiber, 10% of vitamin A, 14% of thiamin (B1), 18% of riboflavin (B2), 13% of folate, 11% of iron, 13% of phosphorus, 15% of potassium, and 12% of selenium.

Cobbler:
1 (12 ounce) can evaporated fat-free milk
2 whole vanilla beans
5 ½ cups under-ripe banana slices (about 6 bananas)
½ cup brown sugar

1 (16 ounce) bag frozen, unsweetened strawberries, thawed
1 (8 ounce) can crushed pineapple, in its own juice
1 ½ cups all-purpose flour
1 ½ cups sugar
2 teaspoons baking powder
½ teaspoon salt
½ teaspoon cinnamon

Topping:
½ cup sugar
½ cup all-purpose flour
1 tablespoon fat-free margarine
½ cup chopped macadamia nuts
12 servings of low-fat vanilla ice cream (½ cup per serving)

Combine evaporated milk and vanilla beans in a medium sauce pan. Cover and cook on low heat for about 15 minutes (do not simmer). Remove from pan from heat. Remove beans from milk, cut in half, and then slice each piece in half length-wise. Use a spoon to scrape the tiny black seeds from the inside of each bean, and add the seeds to the milk.

Add the brown sugar and bite-sized banana slices to the milk. Stir, cover, and cook on low heat for 45 minutes, stirring once or twice. Milk should be almost reaching a simmer at the end of the 45 minutes (do not simmer or boil). Remove from heat. Add strawberries and pineapple to the bananas and milk, stirring gently.

Preheat oven to 325°. Spray a 13x9-inch pan with cooking spray and wipe with a paper towel to spread evenly and absorb the excess.

In a large bowl, combine remaining cobbler ingredients and mix well. Gently stir the fruit and milk mixture into the large bowl until well mixed. Pour into pan.

For the crumb topping, combine the sugar and flour. Add the margarine to make crumbs. Stir in the nuts. Sprinkle evenly over cobbler. Bake for 50 minutes.

Serve warm with ½ cup of ice cream per serving.

Nutritional information per serving (based on 12 servings – cobbler plus ice cream):

The Basics	Power Punch	% Daily Value
Calories 495	Vitamin B6 (0.4 mg)	21%
Protein 8 g	Calcium (250 mg)	25%
Carbohydrate 104 g	Manganese (0.4 mg)	22%
Total fat 6 g	Strawberries (38 g)	
% Calories from fat 11		
Saturated fat 2 g		
Dietary Fiber 5 g		
Cholesterol 5 mg		
Sodium 278 mg		

Sweet Potato Soufflé
Makes 8 Servings

This is a great dessert or side-dish. In addition to the Power Punch nutrients listed below, each serving is a good source of the following (based on percent of Daily Values): 12% of protein, 17% of fiber, 14% of thiamin (B1), 14% of vitamin B6, 10% of folate, 10% of calcium, 10% of iron, 11% of magnesium, 13% of phosphorus, and 16% of potassium.

Filling:
Butter-flavored cooking spray
3 ½ cups cooked, peeled, mashed sweet potatoes
½ cup sugar
3 tablespoons fat-free margarine
½ cup fat-free egg substitute
½ cup evaporated fat-free milk, canned
1 teaspoon vanilla extract

Crumb Topping:
⅓ cup all-purpose flour
1 cup brown sugar
⅛ teaspoon salt
1 ½ tablespoons fat-free margarine
1 cup finely chopped pecans

Bake or microwave the sweet potatoes until cooked completely. Allow to cool

Preheat oven to 325°. Spray a 2-quart casserole pan with cooking spray and wipe with a paper towel to spread evenly and absorb the excess.

Peel the potatoes and mash in a large bowl. Add the remaining filling ingredients and mix well. Spoon into the casserole pan.

115

Combine the flour, sugar, and salt. Add the margarine and mix until crumbs are evenly moist. Add the pecans and mix well. Sprinkle over the sweet potato mixture.

Bake for 35 minutes. Serve hot or cold.

Nutritional information per serving (based on 8 servings):

The Basics	Power Punch	% Daily Value
Calories 388	Vitamin A	390%
Protein 6 g	Riboflavin/B2 (0.4 mg)	25%
Carbohydrate 69 g	Copper (0.46 mg)	23%
Total fat 11 g	Manganese (1.3 mg)	64%
% Calories from fat 25	Sweet Potatoes (87 g)	
Saturated fat 1 g		
Dietary Fiber 4 g		
Cholesterol 0 mg		
Sodium 158 mg		

Almond Pudding
Makes Approximately 11 Servings

This delicious pudding was inspired by a recipe I saw in a Turkish cookbook recommended to us by my husband's friend, Samet. It is very mellow, rich and delicious. In addition to the Power Punch nutrients listed below, each serving is a good source of the following (based on percent of Daily Values): 11% of copper, 18% of magnesium, and 15% of potassium.

Ingredients:
1 cup almond butter
3 (12-ounce each) cans evaporated fat-free milk
6 tablespoons cornstarch
1 cup sugar
2 teaspoons vanilla extract

Note: most grocery stores sell almond butter in the peanut butter and jelly section or in the health food section. If you can't find it there, check with you local health food store.

Combine the almond butter, one can of milk, cornstarch, and sugar in a medium sauce pan and mix well. Add the other two cans of milk and mix well. Bring to a boil over medium heat, stirring almost constantly. Then simmer on low heat for one minute, stirring constantly.

Remove from heat, add vanilla, and mix well. Pour into small, dessert serving bowls. Makes about 5 ½ cups.

Nutritional information per serving (based on 11 servings; ½ cup each serving):

The Basics	Power Punch	% Daily Value
Calories 318	Protein (10 g)	20%
Protein 10 g	Riboflavin/B2 (0.5 mg)	28%
Carbohydrate 40 g	Vitamin D (78 IU)	20%
Total fat14 g	Vitamin E (7 IU)	23%
% Calories from fat 38	Calcium (325 mg)	33%
Saturated fat 1 g	Manganese (0.5 mg)	28%
Dietary Fiber 1 g	Phosphorus (319 mg)	32%
Cholesterol 0 mg		
Sodium 134 mg		

Butter Pecan Ice Cream
Makes 12 Servings

The caramelized pecans make this ice cream especially decadent! In addition to the Power Punch nutrients listed below, each serving is a good source of the following (based on percent of Daily Values): 13% of protein, 15% of riboflavin (B2), and 18% of phosphorus.

Ingredients:
1 ⅓ cup chopped pecans
¼ cup fat-free caramel sauce
1 cup fat-free sweetened condensed milk
2 cups evaporated fat-free milk
1 tablespoon fat-free margarine
1 teaspoon vanilla extract

Preheat oven to 350°. Spread pecans on a cookie sheet and drizzle with caramel sauce. Bake about 8 minutes (until bubbly). Cool completely. Combine the remaining ingredients and mix well. Follow your ice cream maker's instructions for making ice cream, adding the pecans at the very end when the ice cream is almost done freezing. Makes about 6 cups, or 12 portions.

Nutritional information per serving (based on 12 servings; ½ cup each serving):

The Basics	Power Punch	% Daily Value
Calories 218	Calcium (199 mg)	20%
Protein 7 g	Manganese (0.6 mg)	30%
Carbohydrate 28 g		
Total fat 10 g		
% Calories from fat 39		
Saturated fat 1 g		
Dietary Fiber 1 g		
Cholesterol 2 mg		

Vanilla Ice Cream
Makes 10 Servings

This recipe couldn't be simpler, and you can vary the flavor by using different flavors of pudding mix. In addition to the Power Punch nutrients listed below, each serving is a good source of the following (based on percent of Daily Values): 14% of protein, 14% of vitamin D, and 10% of potassium.

Ingredients:
¾ cup fat-free sweetened condensed milk
2 (12-ounce each) cans evaporated fat-free milk
1 teaspoon vanilla extract
1 (3.4 oz.) package instant vanilla pudding mix

Combine all ingredients and mix well. Following your ice cream maker's instructions for making ice cream. Makes about 5 cups, or 10 portions

Nutritional information per serving (based on 10 servings; ½ cup per serving):

The Basics	Power Punch	% Daily Value
Calories 162	Riboflavin/B2 (0.3 mg)	20%
Protein 7 g	Calcium (259 mg)	26%
Carbohydrate 33 g	Phosphorus (266 mg)	27%
Total fat 0 g		
% Calories from fat 1		
Saturated fat 0 g		
Dietary Fiber 0 g		
Cholesterol 2 mg		
Sodium 259 mg		

Grape Sherbet
Makes Approximately 11 Servings

If you or your kids like an intense grape flavor, this is the dessert for you. In addition to the Power Punch nutrients listed below, each serving is a good source of the following (based on percent of Daily Values): 15% of riboflavin/B2, 13% of vitamin D, 18% of calcium, and 12% of manganese.

Ingredients:
2 (12-ounce each) cans evaporated fat-free milk
1 (3.4 ounce) package instant lemon pudding mix
1 (11.5 ounce) can 100% grape juice concentrate (juice from purple grapes, not green or white grapes)

Combine pudding mix with one of the cans of milk and mix well. Then add the other can of milk and the can of juice concentrate, and mix well. Following your ice cream maker's instructions for making ice cream. Makes about 5 ½ cups, or 11 portions.

Nutritional information per serving (based on 11 servings; ½ cup per serving):

The Basics	Power Punch	% Daily Value
Calories 155	Vitamin C (31 mg)	52%
Protein 5 g	Phosphorus (202 mg)	20%
Carbohydrate 34 g	Purple grape juice (30 g)	
Total fat 0 g		
% Calories from fat 1		
Saturated fat 0 g		
Dietary Fiber 0 g		
Cholesterol 0 mg		
Sodium 206 mg		

About the Author

Karen was born in and raised near St. Louis, Missouri. She lives with her husband on a small barrier island near Charleston, South Carolina, where they serve at the whims of their four cats.

Power Desserts is Karen's second cookbook. Her dessert creations are a product of her uncompromising sweet tooth and her passion for healthy living. Creating desserts has been a hobby since she was an undergraduate at St. Mary's College in Notre Dame, Indiana. She has a Ph.D. in clinical psychology from the University of South Florida and an M.B.A. from The Citadel.

Karen is currently the Chief Compliance Officer for Discovery Alliance International, Inc. (DAI) and the President of Patient Advocacy Council, Inc., one of DAI's subsidiary companies. DAI is committed to making lives healthier by conducting clinical trials of new treatments and new products and providing ethical review services to oversee the protection of human research participants.

Prior to joining DAI, Karen was an Assistant Professor in the Department of Psychiatry and Behavioral Sciences at the Medical University of South Carolina (MUSC) and Director of the MUSC Medical Center Quality Management department.

Wellness

www.womeninwellness.com

IT'S ALL ABOUT YOU!
fitness…with a twist

What's different about Women in Wellness?

*1. A whole-approach to wellness, covering physical, emotional
and spiritual health*
2. Interactive one-on-one coaching and customized planning
3. Sister in Success support program
*4. We give you points, redeemable for prizes as you reach your
goals!*

change your life with a click…
FREE ONLINE WELLNESS CLUB!

Also available
from Champion Press, Ltd.

by Brook Noel a.k.a. The Rush Hour Cook

The Rush Hour Cook: Family Favorites by Brook Noel $5.95

The Rush Hour Cook: One-Pot Wonders by Brook Noel $5.95

The Rush Hour Cook: Effortless Entertaining by Brook Noel $5.95

The Rush Hour Cook: Presto Pasta by Brook Noel $5.95

The Rush Hour Cook: Weekly Wonders $16

by Deborah Taylor-Hough

Frozen Assets: Cook for a Day, Eat for a Month $14.95
Frozen Assets Lite & Easy: Cook for a Day, Eat for a Month $14.95
Frozen Assets Reader Favorites: Cook for a Day, Eat for a Month $25
Mix and Match Recipes: Creative Recipes for Busy Kitchens $9.95
A Simple Choice: A Practical Guide to Saving Your Time, Money and Sanity $14.95

Also available:

365 Quick, Easy and Inexpensive Dinner Menus by Penny E. Stone (Over 1000 recipes!)

The Frantic Family Cookbook: mostly healthy meals in minutes by Leanne Ely $29.95 hardcover, $14.95 paperback

Healthy Foods: an irreverent guide to understanding nutrition and feeding your family well by Leanne Ely $19.95

The Complete Crockery Cookbook: create spectacular meals with your slow cooker by Wendy Louise $16

Crazy About Crockery: 101 Easy & Inexpensive Recipes for Less than .75 cents a serving by Penny Stone

TO ORDER
read excerpts, sample recipes, order books and more at
www.championpress.com
or send a check payable to Champion Press, Ltd. to 4308 Blueberry Road,
Fredonia, WI 53021. Please include $3.95 shipping & handling for the first item
and $1 for each additional item.

Also available
from Champion Press, Ltd.
visit www.championpress.com

Till We Eat Again: Confessions of a Diet Dropout will be loved by any and all who have attempted to lose weight. Author Judy Gruen tries everything from belly dancing to boot camp, in her attempt to shed pounds before a class reunion. Treat yourself to a laugh!

Healthy Foods: an irreverant guide to understanding nutrition and feeding your family well...Tired of health food that tastes weirder than It looks? Let Leanne Ely change your diet with this part cookbook part nutrition guide. You'll find that not only can healthy eating taste great—it can be easy and enjoyed by kids, too!

Squeezing Your Size 14 Self into a Size Six World: a real-woman's guide to food, fitness and self-acceptance. Plagued with unrealistic expectations, poor body image and an unsuccessful dieting track record, women are still hunting for the "cure" to get the shape they desire.Carrie Myers Smith, a contributing editor for *Energy* Magazine, has been there and learned that life isn't about counting calories or pounds, but about a total wellness program that addresses both internal and external needs of a whole lifetime. (A companion journal/workbook is also available.)